# JavaScript Next

Your Complete Guide to the New Features Introduced in JavaScript, Starting from ES6 to ES9

Raju Gandhi

Apress®

*JavaScript Next*

Raju Gandhi
Columbus, OH, USA

ISBN-13 (pbk): 978-1-4842-5393-9          ISBN-13 (electronic): 978-1-4842-5394-6
https://doi.org/10.1007/978-1-4842-5394-6

Managing Director, Apress Media LLC: Welmoed Spahr
Acquisitions Editor: Louise Corrigan
Development Editor: James Markham
Coordinating Editor: Nancy Chen

Cover designed by eStudioCalamar

Distributed to the book trade worldwide by Springer Science+Business Media New York, 233 Spring Street, 6th Floor, New York, NY 10013. Phone 1-800-SPRINGER, fax (201) 348-4505, e-mail orders-ny@springer-sbm.com, or visit www.springeronline.com. Apress Media, LLC is a California LLC and the sole member (owner) is Springer Science + Business Media Finance Inc (SSBM Finance Inc). SSBM Finance Inc is a **Delaware** corporation.

For information on translations, please e-mail rights@apress.com, or visit http://www.apress.com/rights-permissions.

Apress titles may be purchased in bulk for academic, corporate, or promotional use. eBook versions and licenses are also available for most titles. For more information, reference our Print and eBook Bulk Sales web page at http://www.apress.com/bulk-sales.

Any source code or other supplementary material referenced by the author in this book is available to readers on GitHub via the book's product page, located at www.apress.com/9781484253939. For more detailed information, please visit http://www.apress.com/source-code.

Printed on acid-free paper

*IN MEMORIAM*

*My Baa*

*(1932–2018)*

ભગવાન એમની આત્મા ને શાંતિ આપે

# Table of Contents

# About the Author

**Raju Gandhi** is a programmer with over 20 years of experience in the software industry. He believes that the key to writing software users will cherish lies in having a keen understanding of the problem, as well as intricate knowledge of the tools available to solve those problems. He has been a core speaker on the No Fluff, Just Stuff symposium series for over 7 years, along with other conferences like DevNexus, Connect.Tech, and GIDS, India. In both his careers as a software developer and teacher, he believes the key is to keep things simple, and in the words of Rich Hickey, "de-complected." This approach seems to scale well, for both maintainable software and happy audience members.

# About the Technical Reviewers

**Toby Jee** is a software programmer currently located in Sydney, Australia. He loves Linux and open source projects. He programs mainly in Java, JavaScript, Typescript, and Python. In his spare time, Toby enjoys walkabouts, reading, and playing guitar.

**Venkat Subramaniam** is an internationally recognized polyglot programmer, author, entrepreneur, and a regularly invited speaker at various international conferences. When not hiking the mountains of Colorado, Venkat spends his time as a software consultant for companies around the world, helping them adapt to various technologies and sustainable agile practices.

# Acknowledgments

Writing a book is a solitary pursuit. However, we sit on the shoulders of giants—past, present, and future. This includes our families, teachers, and mentors who have demonstrated to us the value of hard work and discipline, the technologists that came before us who built what we sometimes take for granted, and finally, those who presently work tirelessly to push the envelope and improve the status quo. I know that I have been blessed to have had a chance to be influenced by many such greats—to every one of you reading this book, you know who you are, and what you mean to me. Thank you.

I have had the privilege of speaking at many conferences, though one name in particular stands out, namely, the No Fluff Just Stuff (NFJS) conference circuit. I am indebted to Jay Zimmerman, the director of NFJS, for giving me a shot, as well as the other speakers on the circuit as they continue to provide inspiration and share their experiences. This book is the result of my having the chance to speak on this subject for a while, but the meat of it comes from the interactions I have had with hundreds of smart, talented developers around the world who made me question my own understanding of the concepts, and forced me to dig deeper.

To Brian and Anne Sam-Bodden—my long-time employers, and more importantly, friends—you have always had more faith in my capabilities than I did. You egged me on to become a speaker and encouraged me to write a book. You provided me an environment where I could experiment, and eventually flourish and thrive. I will always remain indebted to you.

A special shout-out to my friend and mentor Dr. Venkat Subramaniam. Venkat is someone I have come to lean on for everything between advice and camaraderie, both personal and professional, and who, despite his frenetic schedule, always manages to find the time to listen to me and provide a fair and unbiased perspective (often using Dad jokes, but they get the job done).

To all the folks at Apress who made this book a reality, including Louise Corrigan, Nancy Chen, and James Markham—thank you for your patience and hard work. It has been a pleasure.

Despite the best efforts of all those involved in reviewing, editing, and proofreading this book, any and all omissions and mistakes are mine, and mine alone.

ACKNOWLEDGMENTS

I would like to express my love and appreciation toward my significantly better half, Michelle. She patiently took care of everything our lives threw at us, including taking care of our boys, Mason and Micah, as I played recluse to work on this book. Of course, I would be remiss if I did not mention our other two "children"—Buddy, our yorkie-poodle, and Skye, our labradoodle—for providing unflinching companionship and endless amounts of entertainment. Special thanks to my parents and sisters, who will never admit to it but have been the catalyst in forming me into who I am.

Last, but certainly not the least, I tip my hat off to you, the reader. Your attention is a scarce resource, and I appreciate the time you will spend with this book. Happy learnings.

# Introduction

JavaScript is everywhere—it runs single-page applications on the client side, is used on the server side (with technologies like Node.js), helps build desktop applications with Electron,[1] and can be used to work with single-board computers like Raspberry Pi.[2] JavaScript is even used to train machine-learning models in the browser using technologies like TensorFlow.js.[3] All this to say, JavaScript is (arguably) the most deployed language in the world—every desktop and laptop and every phone with an embedded browser can run JavaScript. As it stands today, JavaScript exhibits many of the features that one would expect from a language with this large a footprint.

But that wasn't always the case.

JavaScript has a long history, spanning 24 years at the time of this writing. In this time, JavaScript went from being a scripting language used to animate web pages to one that is being used everywhere, and for everything. JavaScript's reputation, however, preceded itself—it was deemed quirky and error-prone, and not all the criticisms were without merit. And everyone, including the TC39,[4] the central committee that is responsible for evolving JavaScript, took notice.

In 2015, ES6 was announced, which introduced a slew of new features and syntactic changes to the language. The aim was simple—to usher JavaScript into the modern Web era—armed with the features that developers were vying for, and provide the basis for future editions of the language.

The result? A language that aims to improve developer experience, with constructs that seem familiar to developers coming in from other languages. Alongside, a yearly cadence for releasing future editions was announced, ensuring that JavaScript continues to evolve and mature.

---

[1]https://electronjs.org
[2]www.raspberrypi.org/
[3]www.tensorflow.org/js
[4]https://tc39.es/

Features like default parameters, support for variadic functions, destructuring syntax, and fat-arrow functions make it easier to lean into JavaScript's functional nature, allowing for code that is concise and elegant. Simultaneously, the newly added class syntax makes it possible to build inheritance hierarchies easily, allowing for library and framework authors to provide the necessary "trellis" to hook into, and extend.

Asynchronous programming is a natural consequence of JavaScript's inherent design, and once again, the new additions to JavaScript make things easier. Promises are now a native API, opening the door for a whole new level of abstractions, that we, the developers, can build on. Two such abstractions are async/await, which use promises and help make writing asynchronous code seem almost imperative.

And there is much more! All put together, JavaScript today feels like a very different language—one that acts and behaves like other languages that developers might be used to.

This book aims to introduce you to all of these features, endeavoring to provide a nuanced view of the "what" and the "why" for every inclusion. However, we cannot learn without doing—so this book provides a slew of examples, each one catered to highlight a specific feature. So, let's put our developer hats on, fire up our editors, and write some code.

Ready? Set? Go!

# Who should read this book

This book is directed toward programmers, developers, technical leads, architects, programming hobbyists, or anyone interested in learning about how JavaScript has evolved over the past 5 years. If you are someone who dreads JavaScript development because you have been burnt one too many times by the language, then perhaps this book will demonstrate how the language has been transformed to be more familiar (to programmers comfortable with other languages) and less idiosyncratic.

# What you'll find in this book

This book aims to be a comprehensive resource on all the enhancements that were introduced in Ecmascript (ES) 6, 7, 8, and 9. Every chapter starts with highlighting a deficiency or defect in the language, and its implications. It then introduces a new feature or addition to the language, and how the change addresses the specific problem area.

This book does **not** aim to introduce new features chronologically (starting with edition 6 all the way through 9); rather, I aim to collate features from multiple editions, as long as they logically "reside" together. However, I do highlight which edition the feature was introduced.

Many technical books give you a play-by-play, chapter-by-chapter breakdown of what you are to find in the book. Truth be told, I have always found myself skipping over the listing, preferring to stick to the table of contents, or heading straight for the index to find what I am looking for. Consequently, I am going to save myself a few keystrokes, and you a little time. I do hope you will understand, and perhaps forgive this omission.

## What you won't find in this book

This book does not intend to be a comprehensive resource to programming, or JavaScript, the language. It assumes that you, the reader, have a background in programming and a certain familiarity with the language. However, there are parts to the language that many of us may not have explored in the past, and for those aspects, I do provide a richer discourse if I deem it necessary.

JavaScript also regularly sees modifications, additions, and the occasional deprecation to existing APIs, and this trend continues in the newer editions of the language. Again, this book does not cover any of these; rather, it focuses on *syntactic* enhancements to the language.

Finally, there exist several options to run modern JavaScript. These include transpilers like Babel.[5] This book makes no attempt to cover how to use any such tooling, or document the associated configurations.

## How to use this book

The examples in this book are written with two mandates—they should be bite-sized and should build on previously learned material. In this regard, I believe I have (mostly) succeeded. You can find all the examples in this book in our online repository located at `https://github.com/Apress/javascript-next`. Feel free to clone or download this repository, and then follow the instructions on usage in the README contained therein.

---

[5]`https://babeljs.io/`

Alternatively, the path of least resistance is to simply use your browser console. Most modern browsers, like Chrome[6] and Firefox,[7] come equipped with a console.[8] You can simply copy and paste the examples found in this book in the console and experiment to your heart's desire.

Personally, I prefer to experiment in my text editor. If you are anything like me, and prefer using a familiar medium, you will need Node.js installed. Follow the instructions on their web site[9] to install Node. If you already have Node installed and do not wish to introduce a conflict, investigate "Node Version Manager"[10] or "nvm-windows"[11] that allow you to install multiple versions of Node simultaneously.

Once Node is installed, create a scratch directory anywhere on your computer and navigate to it. Then create a new file named `hello-world.js` with the following contents:

```
console.log('Hello JavaScript!');
```

Switch to the terminal, navigate to your scratch directory, and execute the following command:

```
node hello-world.js
```

You should see the following output:

```
Hello JavaScript!
```

You can run all the examples in this book in this manner. This modus operandi will serve you well, except for Chapter 12, where we talk about modules, wherein I provide additional instructions.

Most editors allow for a way to execute code from within the editor itself using extensions, plugins, or via a build system. Be sure to read the documentation of your favorite editor to see how to enable this to allow for a quick feedback loop. Regardless of the mechanism you employ, ensure that you are always using the correct version of Node.

Let's write some modern JavaScript!

---

[6]`www.google.com/chrome/`

[7]`www.mozilla.org/en-US/firefox/`

[8]In Google Chrome this can be found under View ➤ Developer ➤ JavaScript Console. In Mozilla Firefox use Tools ➤ Web Developer ➤ Web Console.

[9]`https://nodejs.org/en/`

[10]`https://github.com/nvm-sh/nvm`

[11]`https://github.com/coreybutler/nvm-windows`

# `let` and `const` — The New Declarations on the Block

The use of variables in JavaScript, like in many other languages, is pervasive. Assignments, arguments to function calls, and results of computations; variables are everywhere. Simply put, they allow us to store the "state" of a program.

JavaScript only offers one mechanism to *declare* variables, the ubiquitous `var`. However, as we will see in this chapter, `var` presents us with several semantic potholes. We will also see how the introduction of two new keywords, namely `let` and `const`, to declare variables helps us avoid subtle bugs, and often unintended side effects, as well as makes the intent of our code clearer.

By the end of this chapter, we will have seen why `let` and `const` are not only the preferred way to declare and initialize variables, but also have a strong argument in favor of deprecating `var`. We will also learn how to refactor our existing code to reap the benefits that `let` and `const` offer and recognize the best use-case for each.

## The Dangers of Variable Scoping

JavaScript supports both statements and expressions, and typically, to capture the value that results from an evaluation, we use variables. There are times though when a variable, despite its name, isn't a variable, but designated to be a constant. That is, once set, we *intend* for the value of the variable to not change over time.

However, up until now, JavaScript provided us with only one keyword, namely `var`, to initialize variables, regardless of whether they were to see their values change (consider the index in a `for` loop), or be constant. For the latter, developers resorted to a naming convention, typically upper-snake-case, like `SOUTH_WEST`, alluding that it be treated like a constant, with no runtime support from the language.

1

© Raju Gandhi 2019
R. Gandhi, *JavaScript Next*, https://doi.org/10.1007/978-1-4842-5394-6_1

Thus, not only was the use of var overloaded, to add insult to the injury, it presented us with a few stumbling blocks. Variables declared with var are automatically hoisted to the top of the current scope. Furthermore, redeclaring two vars with the same name in the same scope does not throw an error. Combine these two, and the result can prove to be rather insidious as demonstrated here:

```
function insidious() {
  var functionScoped = 'Outer declaration'; ①
  if (true) {
    var functionScoped = 'Inner declaration'; ②
  }
  console.log(functionScoped); ③
  return functionScoped;
}
// prints 'Inner declaration'
insidious();
```

① A top level variable declaration

② Seemingly "shadows" the outer declaration

③ Turns out, the two variables are one and the same!

One *may* assume that the inner nested functionScoped is scoped within the if block, which is **not** true! In fact, the second declaration of functionScoped is a no-op. *However,* this does not prevent JavaScript from declaring the variable *once* (at the top) and then reassigning the value of the variable further down, as reflected in the output. To avoid any confusion, JavaScript developers tend to declare all the variables that are to be used within a function upfront.

This notion of vars not being block scoped is certainly surprising, since many languages scope variables *lexically.* That is, the variable in these languages is scoped textually within the enclosing parentheses, and not visible outside of the scope created by the block. This might lean one to believe that vars are scoped, when in reality they are not, and can have inexplicable outcomes. Consider the following example:

```
function simulateDom() {
  var pseudoDom = {
    button1: {},
```

```
    button2: {},
    button3: {},
  }; ①

  for (var i = 1; i <= 3; i++) {
    var element = pseudoDom['button' + i];
    element.click = function () {
      return 'Item ' + i + ' is clicked.'; ②
    };
  }

  console.log(pseudoDom.button1.click());
  console.log(pseudoDom.button2.click());
  console.log(pseudoDom.button3.click()); ③
  return pseudoDom;
}
// prints 'Item 4 is clicked.' 3 times
simulateDom();
```

    ① Simulate the DOM with three buttons

    ② For each button, add a `click` handler

    ③ All print `Item 4 is clicked`

Since the variable i is hoisted *outside* the `for` loop, and is not local to the `for` loop itself, every click handler "sees" the same i. At the end of the loop, the value of i is predictably 4, which is reported on any button click.

Summarizing, any `var` declared within a function is scoped to that function, even if it *is* defined within a block.

## WHAT ABOUT STRICT MODE?

ES5 introduced `strict` mode as an opt-in feature as a way to restrict some JavaScript behavior. This was done in part to make the transition to future versions of JavaScript easier, by changing the semantics of the code and in particular disallowing some behaviors. While `strict` mode does help prevent some rather nasty errors from occurring, for example, inadvertently declaring "global" variables (variables declared within functions without the `var` keyword), it does **not** change the scoping rules that we have discussed so far.

3

Using `strict` mode with ES5 code is **highly** encouraged, and as we embark on a journey to understand and adopt ES6+, it would be prudent to incrementally introduce `strict` mode in our existing scripts. This will certainly make converting them to ES6 easier. The documentation for `strict` mode is available at `https://developer.mozilla.org/en-US/docs/Web/JavaScript/Reference/Strict_mode`.

In summary, if all the above makes your head spin, then you are not alone. Navigating JavaScripts scoping rules is hard enough; combining that with var-iable hoisting further muddies the waters. In order to address some of the concerns surrounding `vars`, ES6 activated[1] `let`. `let` addresses many of the scoping deficits that come with `var` as we will see in the following sections.

Why `let` instead of simply fixing `var` you might ask. Well, we wouldn't want to go about breaking the Internet, would we?

# let

As you might have surmised, most of the confusion around `vars` exist because `vars` do not respect "block" scope. A block in JavaScript is a way to collect one or more statements; in other words, they allow us to create a compound statement. Blocks are delimited by a pair of curly brackets, and if you are thinking, "Wait. Looping constructs (like `for` and `while`) and conditional statements (like `if` and `else`) use curly brackets. Are those blocks?" then you are right.

Blocks do not introduce scope. However, ES6 introduces block scope for variables that are defined using the `let` keyword. A variable defined with the `let` keyword will be scoped within the closest enclosing block. In other words, variables defined with the `let` keyword are lexically scoped to the closest enclosing block:

```
function letFunction() {
  // console.log('Before defining block', scopedLet); ①

  if (true) {
    let scopedLet = 'I am scoped within a block!'; ②
  }
```

---

[1]I say activated vs. introduced because let was always a reserved keyword in JavaScript.

```
  // console.log('After defining block', scopedVar); ③
}

// invoke it
letFunction();
```

① A variable declared *within* a block cannot be referenced outside of the block

② A variable declared with the let syntax

③ Like before, the variable is not visible outside of the scope defined by the if block

We can breathe a sigh of relief! Variables declared with the let keyword *seem* to follow the rules of scoping that you are used to coming from other languages, and they do reduce the contextual overhead associated with vars.

Many of the issues (and potential bugs) that arise from the broad-reaching var scope can be averted by using let instead. Let us revisit our earlier example of a simulated DOM and see the effect of using let:

```
function simulateDom() {
  let pseudoDom = {
    button1: {},
    button2: {},
    button3: {},
  };

  for (let i = 1; i <= 3; i++) { ①
    let element = pseudoDom['button' + i];
    element.click = function() {
      return 'Item ' + i + ' is clicked.'; ②
    };
  }

  console.log(pseudoDom.button1.click());
  console.log(pseudoDom.button2.click());
  console.log(pseudoDom.button3.click()); ③
```

5

```
  return pseudoDom;
}
// prints 'Item 1 is clicked.', 'Item 2 is clicked.', 'Item 3 is clicked.'
simulateDom();
```

    ① i is local to the for loop

    ② Since i is a local variable, each handler sees the correct value of i

    ③ Predictably all the click handlers report the correct message

As we can see, variables declared with let do respect the scope of the enclosing block, thus making the code a lot easier to reason about.

Although let does simplify the scoping rules for variables, they too come with a few caveats, as we will see in the following section.

## Let Variables are Hoisted

It turns out that variables declared with let do get hoisted to the top of their enclosing block. *However,* an attempt to reference such a variable *before* it is defined will result in an error. This is a departure from the behavior of var, where we can indeed "see" the variable prior to its definition (except that it evaluates to undefined).

Consider the following example:

```
var foo;
{ ①
  foo = function() {
    console.log('I am', bar); ②
  };

  let bar = 'Bar'; ③
  // invoke it
  // foo(); ④
}
```

    ① Introduce an artificial block

    ② foo references bar before it is declared

    ③ We define bar

    ④ We then invoke foo

We can surmise what happened here. The declaration of bar moved to the top of the enclosing block, allowing it to be used prior to its declaration.

In and of itself, this feature (?) might not seem too troublesome. However, there is another constraint that let presents us with. That is, you are **not** allowed to define two variables in the same scope with the same name (this again is a departure from the behavior of vars). JavaScript will throw a SyntaxError in that scenario.

Perhaps the following example will clarify things:

```
function determineFavoriteDrink(profession) {
  switch (profession) {
    case 'Programmer':
      let drink = 'coffee'; ①
      break
    case 'Yoga instructor':
      let drink = 'tea'; ②
      break;
    default:
      let drink = 'water'; ③
      break;
  }
  return drink;
}
// results in a 'SyntaxError'
console.log(determineFavoriteDrink('Programmer'));
```

① Introduce a variable

② This will throw an error!

③ This too will throw an error

Invocation of the function results in a SyntaxError! The reason is that let simultaneously hoists **and** prevents redefinition of the same variable. This example demonstrates a cautionary tale as we start to migrate our code from using var to let— we cannot simply replace var with let. var may have permitted us to get away with sloppy code; however, let correctly tightens things up, and we must exercise caution to ensure that all is well after refactoring. However, this is also to our benefit—let exhibits reasonable semantics, and this alone should prove sufficient for us to never use var again.

## No More IEFEs

JavaScript's lack of scoping for `vars` often led to the use of creative solutions to create private variables. One of these solutions was the use of an "Immediately Executing Function Expression" or IEFE. Let us take a before and after version of the same functionality, one using `vars` with an IEFE and one using `let` with blocks:

```
const counter = (function createCounter() { ①
  var steps = 0; ②
  function increment() {
    steps++;
  }
  function getCount() {
    return steps;
  }

  return {
    increment: increment,
    getCount: getCount,
  }; ③
}());
// use it
// console.log(steps); ④
counter.increment(); ⑤
console.assert(counter.getCount() === 1); ⑥
```

　　① Introduce artificial block by creating an anonymous function

　　② This `var` will be scoped within the declared function

　　③ Expose a public API by `return`-ing an object

　　④ This will result in a `ReferenceError`

　　⑤ You can use the public API

　　⑥ Invoke the public getter

　　With `let` we no longer have to use an IEFE because we can simply surround our code with curly brackets to create an enclosing scope!

```
let counter;
```

8

```
{ ①
  let steps = 0; ②
  let increment = function () { ③
    console.log('increment');
    steps++;
  };
  let getCount = function () {
    return steps;
  };
  counter = {
    increment: increment,
    getCount: getCount,
  }; ④
}
// use it
// console.log(steps); ⑤
counter.increment(); ⑥
console.assert(counter.getCount() === 1); ⑦
```

      ① Introduce artificial block using curly brackets

      ② This variable is automatically scoped within the block

      ③ Convert a function statement to a function expression

      ④ Simply assign a variable to be available outside of the block

      ⑤ We still cannot "see" the let-ted variable

      ⑥ But you can use the public API

      ⑦ Invoke the public getter

Both these examples attempt to limit the visibility of the increment and getCount functions. However, leveraging let allows us to eliminate all the ceremony involved with using vars.

# const

ES6 activates another keyword, namely `const`. As the name suggests, this will define a constant. In other words, it defines a variable whose value cannot be changed once they have been declared.

Other than the fact that `const`s cannot be reassigned, everything we have discussed so far about `let` applies to `const` as well—they have block scope, and will be hoisted to the top of the enclosing block, and we cannot declare two consts with the same name in the same scope.

It is important for us to bear in mind that it is the *binding* of a `const` variable that cannot be changed. This has significance because JavaScript objects (such as `Object` and `Array`) are inherently mutable. Which is to say, if a `const` were assigned a reference to an object, it is that *reference* that cannot be changed; the object itself could change, and the `const` would see that change. Perhaps this is easier seen in code.

```
const VALUE_REFERENCE = 'This cannot be re-assigned'; ①
const ARRAY_REFERENCE = [ 'I', 'am', 'mutable' ]; ②

// attempt re-assignment
// VALUE_REFERENCE = false ③
// ARRAY_REFERENCE = {}

// Mutate the array object
ARRAY_REFERENCE.push('!'); ④
// prints [ 'I', 'am', 'mutable', '!' ]
console.log(ARRAY_REFERENCE);
```

① A value reference

② An object reference

③ Reassignment fails with a `TypeError`

④ We can however mutate the referenced object

---

**WHAT ABOUT IMMUTABLE OBJECTS?**

---

`const` constraints itself to make the binding of a variable immutable. If we want to make an object type in JavaScript immutable, we should consider "freezing" it with say `Object.freeze`, or consider using a library like Immutable.js.[2]

---

Another point of note is declaring a `const` with no initial value also results in a `SyntaxError`. Essentially declaring such a `const` will permanently assign the constant to `undefined`, which is redundant considering JavaScript already has the `undefined` keyword for such situations.

Finally, the JavaScript community has converged around the convention of naming constant variables using upper case with underscores. This makes it easier to identify constants within the codebase.

# The Case for var in ES6 and Beyond

We now know that we can use `let` anywhere we use `var` and get some added benefits like clearer scoping rules. `const`s allow us to declaratively define immutable bindings. Considering we have block scope, we can move away from ceremony like IEFEs for encapsulation. All this to say that for any code written using ES6+, we **should not** be using `var`s anymore.

I suggest we take this a step further—we should be finding ways to write our code in a manner that uses `const` more than `let`. Reassigning variables makes it hard to read, understand, and reason about our code. Given a choice between `let` and `const`, I highly encourage to pick the latter, and you will soon realize how clearer and cleaner the result is.

Tools like ESLint can be configured[3] to error when linting ES6+ code, and it is highly recommended that we do so. `var` will forever remain a part of JavaScript's history; however, it is time for us to move on to using only `let` and `const` in our codebases.

---

[2]https://immutable-js.github.io/immutable-js/
[3]https://eslint.org/docs/rules/no-var

# Summary

ES6 gives us several new constructs to declare and use variables in our code. `let` and `const` allow us to use a declaration style which are more in tune with what we may be used to in other languages. Their scoping rules permit easier reasoning of the code, preventing bugs that often get introduced due to `var`s. As browser vendors offer us better support for ES6 and beyond, it behooves us to embrace these new constructs. Going forward, there is **no** reason to favor `var` anymore. `let` and `const` give us everything we need, with the appropriate checks baked into the runtime. We should leverage linting tools that allow us to enforce this, both at development time and during our continuous builds.

In the next chapter, we will see another revolutionary change that landed in ES6, namely a new syntax to define functions.

# CHAPTER 2

# Lambdas with Arrow Functions

Functions are used everywhere in JavaScript. A face-lift to make their syntax succinct, and consequently easier to use and understand, was long overdue.

JavaScript is, at its core, a functional programming language. It supports functions as first-class citizens, in that they are like any other type in the language. Functions can be assigned to variables, supplied as arguments to other functions, and be return-ed from functions just like we would any other type in JavaScript. JavaScript is also single-threaded. Well-designed APIs and libraries that involve long-running operations work asynchronously, typically accepting a callback which is to be invoked when the (asynchronous) task is complete. These callbacks happen to be functions as well. Finally, the mechanism to define methods on objects also happen to be functions.

In this chapter we will get acclimated with a new syntax for function expressions, also referred to as "arrow" functions that was introduced in ES6. We will see how our code can be made eloquent with shorter syntax, thereby allowing us to express our intent clearly. Our discussion will include how arrow functions' behaviors differ from regular functions, allowing us to discern when best to use arrow functions. By the end of this chapter, you will be raring to return to your codebase knowing that you can confidently eliminate any unnecessary verbosity, leaving behind, well ... let's just call it poetry, shall we?

## Reevaluating the Verbosity of Function Definition

In ES5 we can define functions using several constructs, the two primary mechanisms being function statements and expressions. The focus of this chapter will be on function expressions; however, it behooves me to elaborate on the syntactical difference between the two. Consider the following function *statement*.

© Raju Gandhi 2019
R. Gandhi, *JavaScript Next*, https://doi.org/10.1007/978-1-4842-5394-6_2

```
function identity(n) { ①
  return n;
}
// invoke it
console.assert(identity(42) === 42);

// inspect it
console.assert((typeof identity) === 'function'); ②
console.assert(identity.name === 'identity'); ③
```

      ① A function statement

      ② Prints function

      ③ Prints identity

The function statement requires that a name be provided to the newly created function; otherwise, how would we invoke it later? As we can see from our inspection of the newly defined function, it *is* of type function. Functions are objects of type Function, and correspondingly have properties we can interrogate, such as their names and length.[1]

Now we will take a look at the same function, this time defined using a function expression.

```
const identity = function(n) { ①
  return n;
};

// invoke it
console.assert(identity(42) === 42);

// inspect it
console.assert((typeof identity) === 'function'); ②
console.assert(identity.name === 'identity'); ③
```

      ① A function expression

      ② Prints function

      ③ Prints identity

---

[1] length being the number of arguments that the function expects.

As we can see, this too defines a function that behaves identical to the one we defined using a statement. Rather than supplying a name to the function, we assign the value of the expression to a variable, or in this case, a `const`. This function is identical to and consequently behaves identically to a function defined using a statement.

The difference, however, lies in how they are loaded. Function statements are loaded before any of the code is executed. This means that you can define a function statement anywhere, and use it anywhere—you can even invoke the function before defining it as a function statement. On the other hand, function expressions involve assignments to variables, which, as we know from a previous chapter, are subject to hoisting rules. Therefore, using the variable *before* it is assigned to a function expression will result in an error. Observe:

```
 // invoke it before defining it
fnStatement(); ①
function fnStatement() { ②
  console.log('I am a function statement');
}
// invoke it
fnStatement();
// fnExpression(); ③

const fnExpression = function () { ④
  console.log('I am a function expression');
};
// invoke it
fnExpression();
```

> ① Using a function defined as a statement before it is actually defined is allowed
>
> ② A function statement
>
> ③ Using a function defined as an expression before it is actually defined results in an error
>
> ④ A function expression

Choosing between defining functions as statements and expressions is largely a matter of taste. But considering function expressions permit us to omit the function name they tend to be a little less verbose than their statement counterparts.

However, at times even this relatively succinct function expression syntax can often prove to be rather verbose. Consider a scenario wherein we attempt a series of operations on the elements of `Array` to derive a final value:

```
const nums = [1, 2, 3, 4, 5];

const result = nums
            .map(function(n) {
              return n * 3; ①
            })
            .filter(function(n) {
              return (n % 2) === 0; ②
            })
            .reduce(function(acc, n) {
              return acc + n; ③
            }, 0);
```

① Triple every number in the array

② Filter out even numbers only

③ Reduce the result to its sum

This example may be trite; however, it does highlight the ceremony involved in writing even the simplest of functions. As a result, it becomes difficult to parse out what we are *actually* attempting to accomplish. This often leads developers to extracting the callbacks into (named) function statements, which are not only more verbose, but end up dispersing the code, making it even harder to understand what it is we are trying to accomplish.

Arrow functions to the rescue!

# Arrow Functions

Arrow functions (sometimes referred to as "fat" arrow functions—you will see these terms used synonymously) present us with a much more concise syntax for function definitions. Let us start by exploring the syntax of arrow functions.

# Syntax

Arrow functions eliminate a lot of the verbosity that function expressions present. Let us whet our appetite with a simple example:

```
const doubleIt = n => n * 2;

// invoke it
console.assert(doubleIt(8) === 16);
```

Let us feast our eyes on the elegance of arrow functions prior to delving into the weeds. Gone is the `function` keyword, the parentheses, the curly brackets, and the `return` keyword. (The last true are not entirely true, as we will see in the following discussion.) All that remains is the **true** intent of the function.

As we can see, much like function expressions, we do not provide a name for the function itself. Rather we assign the result of *evaluating* the expression to a variable so that we can reference it later.

Now that we have had a taste of arrow functions, let us discuss some syntactical details.

## Parentheses or No Parentheses?

Arrow functions have their parameters listed to the left of the fat arrow. It is permitted to skip the parentheses **if and only if** the function signature has one parameter.[2] The following snippet offers the various permutations allowed for arrow function parameters:

```
const noop = () => {}; ①
const identity = n => n; ②
const get = (obj, k) => obj[k]; ③
```

> ① Zero-parameter list requires parenthesis
>
> ② Single-parameter list makes the parenthesis optional
>
> ③ Two or more parameters require the parenthesis

---

[2]Though strictly speaking this is the only time we can skip the parentheses. The use of default and variable arguments which we will see soon also forces us to use parentheses with arrow functions.

This discussion begs the question, does skipping the parenthesis for single-parameter arrow functions buy us anything? The convention adopted widely across the JavaScript community is one where we should skip the parenthesis if we can. In other words, while it may seem to go against the notion that single-argument arrow statements should be syntactically consistent (with no-arg and multi-arg arrow functions), it does reduce the verbosity especially in the case of higher-order functions as we will see soon.

The right-hand side of the arrow function syntax offers a little more subtlety as we will see now.

## Expression and Statement Bodies

All the examples we have seen so far have had single-line bodies. What if our function had to do a little more work?

It turns out we can indeed use curly brackets to define the function body. However, as you might recall, curly brackets create blocks in JavaScript, which are statements, not expressions! In other words, every example we have seen so far used an expression as its body, thus alleviating the need to explicitly `return` from the function. If we are to switch to using blocks (which is a statement and therefore is not *evaluated*), then we are forced to explicitly `return` from the function. (Otherwise, the function, like any regular function, returns an implicit `undefined`.) Let us define a multiline-bodied arrow function:

```
const reducer = (acc, n) => { ①
  acc.push(n);
  return acc; ②
};

// invoke it
console.log(reducer([2, 3], 1)); // prints '[ 2, 3, 1 ]'
```

① Use curly brackets to start body

② Explicit return required

It *is* recommended that if we are to use curly brackets, we should have explicit returns in the body. Not doing so can prove to be rather baffling. Observe:

```
const confuser = () => { profession: 'JS Ninja' };
// invoke it
console.log(confuser());
```

Quick! What does the function return upon invocation? Is it an object with one key, or is that a block with a `label` and therefore returns `undefined`? As you can see, the overloaded nature of curly brackets to define blocks *and* objects causes confusion in conjunction with the arrow syntax.

It turns out that if JavaScript "sees" curly brackets in an arrow function definition it treats it as if it were a block body. This means that upon invocation, this function will return `undefined`.

What if we indeed wanted to return an object? We have two options—explicitly use a block with a `return` or wrap the body in parenthesis, like so:

```
const confuserOne = () => ({ profession: 'JS Ninja' });
// prints '{ profession: 'JS Ninja' }'
console.log(confuserOne());

// alternatively
const confuserTwo = () => {
 return { profession: 'JS Ninja' };
};
// prints '{ profession: 'JS Ninja' }'
console.log(confuserTwo());
```

That sums up all the syntactical nuances of arrow functions. Now let us consider the semantic differences between arrow functions and regular functions. But before we go there, we must take a brief digression into regular functions, and how they work with `this`.

## Regular Functions Dynamically Set `this`

When a regular function (defined using function statements or expressions) references `this`, that reference is resolved dynamically based on the *invocation pattern* used:

```
'use strict';

const returnsThis = function () {
  return this;
};
```

19

```
var obj1 = {
  name: 'obj1',
  method: returnsThis, ①
};
```

```
console.assert(obj1.method() === obj1); ②
```

```
var obj2 = {
  name: 'obj2',
};
```

```
console.assert(returnsThis.apply(obj2) === obj2); ③
console.assert(returnsThis() === undefined); ④
```

① Set a property that references a local function in scope

② Invoke the function using the "method invocation" pattern

③ Use the "apply invocation" pattern

④ Invoke the function using the "function invocation" pattern

I must emphasize that we are running the code in strict mode to avoid the automatic boxing that "nonsecure" environments tend to enforce.[3] That said, we then invoke the same function using three different invocation patterns[4] to see the value of this be different in each case!

We first assign a property on an object to point to the local function, and then invoke it like we would any other function property on that object using the "dot" operator. As we might expect, this points to whatever is on the left of the "dot" at invocation time. In other words, it points to the "current context."

We then use the apply (or its cousin call) which effectively sets the this inside the function prior to invoking it. Another way to think about it is that this line is equivalent to the method invocation pattern, except we are setting this using apply instead of being forced to tack on a new property on the object.

---

[3]https://developer.mozilla.org/en-US/docs/Web/JavaScript/Reference/Strict_mode #Securing_JavaScript

[4]The fourth invocation pattern is the "constructor invocation" pattern. However, these three invocations suffice to make our case here.

Finally, we simply invoke the function without any context—that is, we do not invoke the function on any object; in `strict mode` the function simply returns `undefined`, which is what one would expect.

As we can see, `this` within a function expression (or statement) is set at the time of invocation, *not* at the time of definition. This is where the behavior of "regular" functions diverges from that of arrow functions. While regular functions dynamically set the meaning of `this` at invocation time, arrow functions bind it lexically; in other words, arrow functions bind `this` at *definition* time.

## Lexically Bound `this`

Arrow functions do not set the meaning of `this` upon invocation. Rather they set or "cement" it to whatever `this` evaluates to when they are created. Consider the following:

```
'use strict';

const GLOBAL_OBJECT = this; ①
const returnMe = () => this; ②

var obj1 = {
  name: 'obj1',
  method: returnMe,
};
console.assert(obj1.method() === GLOBAL_OBJECT); ③

var obj2 = {
  name: 'obj2',
};
console.assert(returnMe.apply(obj2) === GLOBAL_OBJECT); ④
console.assert(returnMe() === GLOBAL_OBJECT); ⑤
```

① Grab a handle to the global object in scope so we `assert` against it

② Define an arrow function that simply `returns this`

③ Trying to use it as a method does not change the context

④ Neither does `apply`

⑤ Regular functions would have returned `undefined` here (as we have seen)

Defining an arrow function seems to be the same as defining a regular function, and bind-ing `this` to whatever is `this` at definition time! And indeed, this is the case.

Let us look at some more caveats that apply to arrow functions.

## Other Caveats

Arrow functions differ from regular functions in other subtle ways. Due to the internal implementation of arrow functions, they cannot be used as constructor functions. If we wish to define a constructor function, we must continue using regular functions.

Another difference is that `this` is not the only thing that is lexically bound. When a function defined as an expression or statement is invoked, JavaScript creates an object that captures all of the arguments supplied to the function at invocation time. This object, named `arguments,` is available within the function body. However, arrow functions do not get an `arguments` object. However, `strict mode` restricted the API surface area of arguments, and ES6 provides us with variable arguments (which we will see soon), further reducing the need for `arguments` so this does not present itself as much of a caveat. Let us take a look at a quick example to see how this works:

```
function PersonAsRegularFunction(name) { ①
  this.name = name;
}
const nate = new PersonAsRegularFunction('Nate'); ②
// prints { name: 'Nate' }
console.log(nate);

const PersonAsArrowFunction = (name) => { ③
  this.name = name;
};
// const neal = new PersonAsArrowFunction('Neal'); ④

function regularFunction() {
  return arguments;
}
// prints { '0': 10, '1': 'a', '2': true, '3': false }
console.log(regularFunction(10, 'a', true, false)); ⑤
```

```
const arrowFunction = () => arguments;
// prints 'ReferenceError: arguments is not defined'
// console.log(arrowFunction(10, 'a', true, false)); ⑥
```

① Define a function using a statement

② Invoke a function statement as a constructor which returns successfully

③ Define a function as an arrow function

④ Invoking an arrow function as a constructor throws an error

⑤ Regular functions get an arguments object upon invocation

⑥ Arrow functions on the other hand do not

Let us step back and think about what this means—regular functions dynamically set the value of this at invocation time. Simultaneously, the arguments object is created to capture all of the arguments supplied at invocation time. That is to say, both this and the arguments object when used inside of a function body are *contextual*—they rely on the invocation context so that they can be defined correctly. However, arrow functions cement the value of this at definition time, and are not provided the arguments object at all. In other words, arrow functions are specifically designed to use as little of the context around them as possible. If our function implementation needs to use context defined at runtime, we will be best served using regular functions.

## Use-cases

One might wonder, with all the subtle changes that we must now be aware of, are arrow functions worth it? JavaScript as we have seen is a functional programming language. Using functions as arguments and returning functions from higher-order functions is a very common paradigm in JavaScript. In fact, most Array iteration and manipulation functions tend to be higher-order functions, and present the perfect opportunity for arrow function. Let us revisit our earlier example of map-ing and reduce-ing over an array and see how we can use arrow functions instead.

```
const nums = [1, 2, 3, 4, 5];

const result = nums
                .map(n => n * 3) ①
                .filter(n => (n %  2) === 0) ②
                .reduce((acc, n) => acc + n, 0); ③
```

① Triple every number in the array

② Filter out even numbers only

③ Reduce the result to its sum

First, let us stop for a minute, and consider the elegance of the code. As we can see, gone is all the ceremony, and what remains is the essence of what it is we are trying to accomplish. It is almost as if arrow functions were designed with this intent in mind!

Another use-case is when we know for *certain* what this represents when the arrow function is defined.

```
const neo = {
  friends: [
    'Morpheus',
    'Brian',
    'Switch',
  ],
  addFriends: function () {
    const args = Array.prototype.slice.call(arguments);
    args.forEach(f => this.friends.push(f)); ②
  },
};

// invoke addFriends
neo.addFriends('Niobe', 'Tank'); ①
// prints '[ 'Morpheus', 'Brian', 'Switch', 'Niobe', 'Tank' ]'
console.log(neo.friends);
```

① Set the "context"

② Arrow function works as expected

Here we know that `this` inside `addFriends` will point to the object referenced by the `const neo` because `addFriends` is invoked as a method on `neo`. Therefore, within `addFriends`, we can define an arrow function which can use `this` because this points to the owner object when that arrow function is defined. However, we cannot make `addFriends` itself an arrow function, since at the time the function is defined; `this` points to the global object! As we might conclude, it is best to be certain what `this` points to when referencing it inside an arrow functions, or simply consider using function expressions.

Let us consider another example of using higher-order functions to build a mini domain-specific language (DSL). In this example we will be working with pure functions—that is, functions that only use the arguments supplied to them. That is, they are "stateless," and thus serve as great candidates for us to use arrow functions. This will give us a great opportunity to see how the terseness of arrow functions can serve us.

```
const and = (a, b) => arg => a(arg) && b(arg); ①

const gt10 = n => n > 10; ②
const even = n => n % 2 === 0; ③

const gt10AndEven = and(gt10, even); ④

console.assert(gt10AndEven(15) === false);
console.assert(gt10AndEven(22) === true);
```

① Define a higher-order predicate function

② Test to see if the argument supplied is greater than 10

③ Test to see if the number is an even number

④ Create a function that tests two conditions

Here we define the `and` function, a higher-order predicate function[5] that given two functions, returns a new function. This new function expects one argument, `args`, that is tested against both predicates and returns true if and only if both predicates are satisfied.[6]

---

[5]A predicate function is a function that returns `true` or `false`.

[6]Note that this function delegates to the in-built && operator, which short-circuits. In other words, the order of arguments matters.

We then define two predicates, and use and to create a new function to test if its supplied argument is both greater than 10 and is even.

Once again, we observe that arrow functions allow us to keenly express our intentions, leaving out any superfluous ceremony associated with function expressions.

# Summary

While arrow functions have a passing resemblance to their expression and statement cousins, their role in the new world of JavaScript remains undisputed. They enable us to leverage JavaScripts inherent functional nature, making code more concise, and readable, and unlike regular functions rein in any attempts to make them stateful.

In this chapter we explored the new syntax for fat-arrow functions. We saw how their semantics differ from that of regular functions, and learned the appropriate use-cases where fat-arrow functions best serve us. As long as we remain mindful of the differences in their behavior, arrow functions will serve us well.

In the next chapter we will explore a new mechanism to define function signatures that allow our code to be more expressive, while reducing the amount of error checking that we are so accustomed to doing within our functions.

# CHAPTER 3

# Effective Function Signatures with Default and Rest Parameters

We all realize the pervasive use of functions in JavaScript. Consequently, defining functions and laying out function signatures is one thing we do a lot. Default parameters, a new feature introduced in ES6, provide us the power to improve how we detail our function signatures. They allow us to specify what the value of a parameter to a function ought to be if no value is passed in at invocation time. Along the same vein, rest parameters allow us to express that a function (or method) has no expectation to the number of arguments you can supply it—in other words, they allow us to explicitly declare variadic functions.

In this chapter we will explore the new syntax for both default and rest parameters. We will see how we can write function signatures that provide our consumers incredible flexibility in how they use them, while simultaneously reducing the amount of error checking we have to do internally. By the end of this chapter, we will be left wondering how we ever managed to work with functions as we know them today!

## Unintentionally Obscuring Intent with Arguments

JavaScript function signatures only include the name of the function. This diverges from many other languages where the signature includes the return type and the parameter list. Since JavaScript is dynamically typed, functions do not declare their return type. However, the part that is most relevant to our discussion here is that the parameter list does not participate in the function signature either. This is the reason

© Raju Gandhi 2019
R. Gandhi, *JavaScript Next*, https://doi.org/10.1007/978-1-4842-5394-6_3

why we do not have overloaded functions in JavaScript. Two functions with the same name even with different parameter lists **will** collide, with the one defined later overwriting the previous one.

Furthermore, JavaScript allows functions to be invoked with as few or as many arguments as the caller wishes to supply. This means that despite a functions *formal* signature, also referred to as its "arity," *every* function in JavaScript is a multi-arity function. We can inspect the same as follows:

```
const sayHello = name => 'Hello ' + name;

const buildUrl = (site, protocol) => protocol + '://' + site;

function add( /**args*/ ) { ①
  let result = 0;
  for (const i in arguments) {
    result += arguments[i];
  }
  return result;
}

console.assert(sayHello.length === 1);
console.assert(buildUrl.length === 2);
console.assert(add.length === 0);

// prints 'Hello undefined'
console.log(sayHello()); ②
// prints 'https://jsrocks.com'
console.log(buildUrl('jsrocks.com', 'https', 'non-required argument')); ③
// prints 42
console.log(add(12, 22, 8)); ④
```

> ① Recall that arrow functions do not have an `arguments` object created upon invocation. This forces us to use a function statement
>
> ② Invoke `sayHello` with zero arguments
>
> ③ Invoke `buildUrl` with more arguments than the function expects
>
> ④ Invoke `add` correctly

Here, we define three functions with differing arities. Officially, all three functions report an arity via the `length` property that is available on function objects.

However, as demonstrated, we can invoke any of those functions with as many or as few arguments as we like, and as the outputs suggest, we may or may not get the desired results. It turns out that JavaScript functions can declare the number of arguments they expect to be supplied by formally listing them in their parameter lists. However, there is no check at runtime to ascertain if indeed the function is invoked with the correct number of arguments. Essentially, we can either *assume* that the function will be invoked correctly or be prepared by installing appropriate checks in the implementation in case we don't get all that we expect.

Lastly, in our example `add` *is* a function that is attempting to be multi-arity—that is, it is a function that can indeed consume as many arguments as we supply it. But with no first-class construct in the language to declare this as part of the function signature, we are forced to provide a hint (typically via documentation or a comment as shown) to clients that they can provide additional arguments if they do wish to do so.

Enter default and rest parameters.

# Default Parameters

Default parameters provide us with a mechanism to highlight what a function really needs, and a way to assume some parameters if they are not supplied. Recall that JavaScript does not have any runtime enforcement to ensure that a function is invoked with the correct number of arguments. Therefore, we, the developers, are forced to accommodate for missing arguments in our implementations. Observe:

```
/**
 * Builds a url
 *
 * @param {site} the url (required)
 * @param {protocol} can be http or https (optional) - defaults to http
 * @returns {string}
 */
const buildUrl = (site, protocol) => {
  if (!site) { ①
    throw new Error('site is required');
  }
```

```
  const p = protocol || 'http'; ②
  return p + '://' + site;
};
```

① Enforce that `site` is required by throwing a runtime error

② We can default `protocol`

Here, we attempt to build a more resilient implementation of the `buildUrl` function. However, the fact that `site` is required and `protocol` is optional is now hidden within the confines of its implementation. Documentation can act as an aid—however, as we all know, it is often at best incomplete, and at worst, nonexistent.

Default parameters allow us to express the same like so:

```
const buildUrl = (site, protocol = 'http') => {
  if (!site) {
    throw new Error('site is required');
  }
  return protocol + '://' + site;
};
```

The default value for `protocol` is now explicitly stated in the method signature, signaling what it will be *if* the client decided to skip it. Admittedly the fact that `site` is required still remains implicit; however the fact that the function author could not find a suitable default for it might in itself be telling.

In other words, a quick glance at the signature of this function reveals far more, which previously would have forced the client to peek at the implementation (if that was even possible), look at the docs (if they were available), or play Russian roulette with argument combinations to see what is or isn't possible.

Now that we have default parameters as a first-class construct in the language, tools like EsDocs[1] can even parse out default parameters and automatically highlight them in generated documentation. This makes using this feature even more enticing.

Let us now look at some subtleties of default parameters.

---

[1]`https://esdoc.org/`

# Qualifying and Skipping Defaults

We can default parameters to be the result of any *expression*—assignments, function calls, and even ternary expressions are all fair game. This is particularly useful if the default value is the result of a configuration or environment lookup:

```
const getDefaultConn = () => {
  // look up ENV config
  // return appropriate connection
  // as a default assume localhost
  return {
    host: 'localhost',
    user: 'me',
    password: 'secret',
    database: 'my_db',
  };
};

const query = (sql, conn = getDefaultConn()) => {
  // use connection string and sql here to query db
  // conn.connect();
  // conn.query(sql);
  // conn.close();
  return conn;
};
```

One thing that might not be obvious is that the defaulted parameter gets its default value evaluated upon invocation of the function, rather than when the function is actually defined. This, as we can see, lets us *defer* the value of conn till we actually invoke it.

Another nuance here is that parameters can see previous parameters declared in the function signature, and use them when assigning their own defaults. This is particularly useful especially when we are thinking of polymorphic implementations. Consider the following:

```
const rectangle = (x, y = x) => [x, y]; ①

// prints '[ 2, 2 ]'
console.log(rectangle(2)); ②
```

31

```
// prints '[ 5, 12 ]'
console.log(rectangle(5, 12)); ③
```

> ① Parameters seeing previous parameters
>
> ② Supply only one side to create a square
>
> ③ Supply both sides to create a rectangle

Of course, we can mix and match all of these in interesting ways:

```
const triangle = (a, b = a, c = Math.hypot(a, b)) => [a, b, c];
```

```
// prints '[ 6, 4, 7.211102550927979 ]'
console.log(triangle(6, 4));
// prints '[ 10, 10, 14.142135623730951 ]'
console.log(triangle(10));
```

We must consider what triggers the use of a default parameter. Obviously *not* passing in a parameter triggers it. In other words, passing in "nothing" causes JavaScript to use the default value. If we think about it, undefined in JavaScript is the equivalent of nothing.[2] Thus, given a function, if we do wish to use the default value for a particular argument, passing in undefined in that position *is* equivalent to "skipping" it.

## Usage Considerations

JavaScript's parser allows any combination of default parameters. We might wish to make the default the first parameter of a function leaving the rest to be filled in at invocation time, or alternate between regular and defaulted parameters. While this might seem interesting, its utility for development is rather limited:

```
const filter = (coll = [], predFn) => coll.filter(predFn);
```

```
// prints '[ 30 ]'
console.log(filter([10, 20, 30], n => n > 25));
```

---

[2] Consider a function that does not have an explicit return statement—therefore it returns nothing. Similarly looking up a nonexistent property on an object returns undefined. Alternatively, null implies something *is* defined, but is *explicitly* set to be empty.

We default the `coll` to be an empty array if it is not supplied. However, a `filter` function that does not have a predicate function to filter with is rather meaningless. Furthermore, if we wish to pass in the absolutely necessary predicate function, we are forced to pass in the first argument since we can't skip arguments during function invocation. Of course, one might argue that we could pass in `undefined` as the first argument thus triggering the default, but that only goes to cement the point; that is, the order of parameters in a function signature **still** matters!

By convention, a function's mandatory, and most "important" parameters are listed to the left, followed by those that *may* be optional. This convention is in no way lessened by the use of default parameters. The fact that default parameters can only see parameters to their *left* underscores this argument.

In short, keep required (and potentially those that *cannot* be assumed) arguments to the left, followed by defaulted ones to the right. This helps highlight the fact that some parameters are absolutely necessary, while allowing us to default others based on their values at invocation time. Win–win. Following this convention helps us make our function signatures more descriptive, reducing or even eliminating any guesswork on the behalf of our consumers.

# Rest Parameters

Default parameters work exceptionally well if and when the function expects a fixed number of parameters. We can choose to highlight those that are required, while defaulting some. But what if a function wishes to express that it can accept an indeterminate number of parameters, and that it is indeed able to use them all? This is where rest parameters come into play.

## The Argument Against `arguments`

JavaScript has always had the `arguments` object available within the invocation context to account for "extra" arguments. Let us revisit our earlier example that adds all of the arguments supplied to it:

```
function add( /**args*/ ) {
  let result = 0;
  for (const i in arguments) {
```

```
    result += arguments[i];
  }
  return result;
}
// prints '20'
console.log(add(2, 3, 5, 10));
```

This function expects n arguments, and it consumes all of them to return a result. Does it accomplish what we set out to do? Absolutely. However, in order to express that the function is indeed multi-arity, we must resort to using a comment block, thus hiding this fact in its implementation.

There remain two more palpable drawbacks to using arguments. While arguments respond to the length property, and allow us to use the subscript ([]) operator to reach a specific argument that was supplied, it just so happens that the arguments object is not really an array! If we wish to manipulate the supplied arguments, for example, sort or filter them, we have no choice but to coerce arguments into an array.[3]

The second issue is that the arguments object includes *all* arguments supplied to the function. If the desire is to treat some parameters differently than others, we are required to separate those from everything else.

We can see both these deficiencies highlighted in a simple example that attempts to simulate the boarding of a plane. The plane in our example has a pilot, a crew member, and n-number of passengers. However, we must be sure to treat our most loyal customers first, so we must board them first. Every passenger has a status, and those with higher status should be invited to board *before* those with other statuses. Let us start by writing a simple comparator function that compares two passengers using their statuses, like so:

```
const byStatus = (a, b) => {
  let ret;
  if (a.status === 'platinum' && b.status !== 'platinum') {
    ret = -1;
  } else if (a.status === 'platinum' && b.status === 'platinum') {
    ret = 0;
```

---

[3]We could avoid the use of arguments altogether by forcing our clients to pass in an array, but that is simply passing the buck. Not to mention that the clients still need to be aware that this is indeed a requirement.

```
  } else if (a.status !== 'platinum' && b.status === 'platinum') {
    ret = 1;
  }
  return ret;
};
```

With the comparator function out of the way, we can write our plane boarding algorithm. Notice that we represent our plane as an array, first push-ing the pilot, who boards first, followed by the crew member, followed by the passengers sorted by their individual status:

```
function boardPlane(pilot, crewMember /** , passengers */ ) {
  const plane = [];
  plane.push(pilot); ①
  plane.push(crewMember); ②
  const toArr = Array.prototype.slice.call(arguments); ③
  const passengers = toArr.slice(2, toArr.length); ④
  plane.push(passengers.sort(byStatus)); ⑤
  return plane;
}

const passengerOne = {
  name: 'James',
  status: 'silver',
};

const passengerTwo = {
  name: 'Joseph',
  status: 'platinum',
};

// invoke it
const plane = boardPlane('Amelia', 'Rosemary', passengerOne, passengerTwo);
console.assert(Array.isArray(plane));

// verify pilots and crew board first
console.assert(plane[0] === 'Amelia');
console.assert(plane[1] === 'Rosemary');
```

```
// verify that passengers board by status
console.assert(Array.isArray(plane[2]));
console.assert(plane[2][0] === passengerTwo);
console.assert(plane[2][1] === passengerOne);
```

① Pilot boards first

② Followed by the crew member

③ Coerce `arguments` to an array

④ Discard the first two items since they are already accounted for

⑤ Sort the remaining items in the array using a custom sort function

This works; however, it feels clumsy. All of the drawbacks we have discussed so far rear their ugly heads. First, we have to coerce the `arguments` object into an array so we can eventually `sort` the passengers. Second, the `arguments` object includes all of the arguments supplied to `boardPlane`, so in order to get to the passengers, we are forced to drop the first two (namely the pilot and the crew member) since they have already been accounted for. The `arguments` object does not account for arguments that already have placeholders provided via function parameter names, shifting the onus to the developer to discern between the arguments that have already been captured, and those that represent the "rest" of the arguments.

Alas! If only there was a way to auto-box all "unaccounted for" arguments into an array ...

## The New . . . Syntax

Rest parameters use a new syntax, namely `...argName` in the parameter list. This parameter will collect any arguments supplied in the function invocation that are **not already** accounted for, and wrap them in an `Array` object.

We can now refactor our example to use rest parameters like so:

```
const boardPlane = (pilot, crewMember, ...passengers) => { ①
  const plane = [];
  plane.push(pilot);
  plane.push(crewMember);
```

```
  plane.push(passengers.sort(byStatus)); ②
  return plane;
};

const passengerOne = {
  name: 'James',
  status: 'silver',
};

const passengerTwo = {
  name: 'Joseph',
  status: 'platinum',
};

// invoke it
const plane = boardPlane('Amelia', 'Rosemary', passengerOne, passengerTwo);
console.assert(Array.isArray(plane));
// verify pilots and crew board first
console.assert(plane[0] === 'Amelia');
console.assert(plane[1] === 'Rosemary');
// verify that passengers board by status
console.assert(Array.isArray(plane[2]));
console.assert(plane[2][0] === passengerTwo);
console.assert(plane[2][1] === passengerOne);
```

① Explicitly declare a rest parameter

② Directly invoke array methods on only the remainder arguments

Almost magically, the code is shorter, with its intent clear. There is no unnecessary coercion, and since we no longer have to account for extras like we did for `arguments`, errors like off-by-one are completely eliminated. Instead we get a real array holding all the arguments supplied that make up the "rest" of the arguments. A glance at the function signature tells us all we need to know—this is a multi-arity function, that needs at least two arguments that are aptly named, and potentially a list of passengers.[4]

---

[4]Here's us hoping that there is indeed a list. It's not going to be a very profitable flight otherwise!

Also, we get one added benefit. It is subtle, but let us see if we can spot one more difference between the original and refactored version. See it yet?

Recall that arrow functions do **not** get an `arguments` object created upon invocation. If we *need* to use `arguments,` we are forced to use a regular function expression or statement. However, in this case, we can go back to using the more succinct arrow function for `boardPlane`. Yay!

# The `rest` of the Details (or is it the Details of `rest`?)

Rest parameters are far less nuanced than some of the other features we have discussed so far. If a function uses rest parameters, then this parameter needs to be the last one in the argument list. This makes sense, since it acts as a greedy operator, gobbling up any and all arguments that have not already been accounted for. Declaring a parameter after a rest parameter in a function signature will result in a `SyntaxError.`

A rest parameter unlike regular parameters **cannot** have a default value assigned to it. Rest parameters have an implicit default value, that being an empty array. In other words, if there are no parameters left for the rest parameter to consume, it will default being an array of length 0. This plays out well, since we do not have to do `undefined` checks.

Given that a rest parameter allows us to define a multi-arity function, let us see how it plays with the `length` property of functions. Recall that the `length` property on functions return the formal arity as defined in its signature. Turns out that rest parameters do **not** participate in the arity count for functions.

Functions also do not expose an API to ascertain if a particular function is indeed using rest parameters. While this bodes well with JavaScript's original design of every function being implicitly multi-arity, it also leaves us with no way to programmatically discover if the last parameter is a rest parameter.

Finally, we come to rest parameters and the `arguments` object. While arrow functions do not get an `arguments` object, regular functions still do. As you might expect, the `arguments` object works just as expected—it gathers up **all** the arguments supplied to a function without considering the fact that the last parameter is a rest parameter.

Let us quickly explore all of this with a trite example:

```
function fnExpression(a, b, ...c) {
  console.log(arguments.length);
}
```

```
const fnArrow = (a, b, ...c) => {
  // do not get an arguments object
};

console.assert(fnExpression.length === 2); ①
console.assert(fnArrow.length === 2); ②
// prints '6'
fnExpression(1, 2, 3, 4, 5, 6); ③
```

① Arity does not include the rest parameter for function expressions

② As well as for arrow functions

③ `arguments.length` reports the total arguments supplied at invocation

# Summary

Default parameters allow us to be more expressive when defining function signatures. They replace superfluous checks with appropriate defaults, thus making our code's intent clearer. Default parameter values are evaluated at invocation time, allowing us to defer the parameter being set within the runtime context of our programs. Since parameters can "see" parameters defined to the left in the function signature, we can make an attempt to make polymorphic functions, and enable the notion of "overloaded" methods as might be used in other languages.

Rest parameters eliminate the need to use the `arguments` object when writing multi-arity functions, with the added benefit of explicit function signature support. This helps remove unnecessary coercions in our code, and provide a mechanism to cleanly capture all arguments not accounted for by parameters.

Neither default nor rest parameters eliminate the need for good API design; in fact they have just the opposite effect. By putting emphasis on parameters that appear on the left with decreasing precedence to the right, they compel us to discern between parameters that are necessary and need be supplied, vs. those that we *might* be able to default.

All of this combined lessens the contextual overheard clients have to bear when using our API. Now, isn't that worth celebrating?

In the next chapter we will look at an improvement targeting JavaScript's inherent mechanism for querying elements of arrays, or values in objects, using the new spread operator and destructuring syntax. These in tandem with default parameters allow us to be even more expressive in our function signatures.

# CHAPTER 4

# Divide and Conquer with Object and Array Destructuring

JavaScript lets us easily create "bags of data" using objects and arrays, permitting us the ability to fluidly wrap data and ship it around in our code. However, the syntax afforded to us to "reach" into these data structures tends to be verbose, imperative, and error-prone. In ES6 and ES9, JavaScript adopts yet another functional construct in the form of the destructuring syntax to improve our experience with unwrapping data, bringing it to parity with how we wrap data in the first place.

In this chapter we will see how the new destructuring syntax for both objects and arrays provide an elegant mechanism to reach into data structures. We will also learn to couple this with our understanding of default and rest parameters, and how these two features work hand in hand to define functions that eloquently express their expectations while being more flexible. By the end of this chapter, we will be safely querying objects and arrays using a clear, succinct, and highly expressive syntax, while improving the way we detail out function signatures.

© Raju Gandhi 2019
R. Gandhi, *JavaScript Next*, https://doi.org/10.1007/978-1-4842-5394-6_4

# Seeking Symmetry Between Structuring and Destructuring

JavaScript offers us two collection-like objects—arrays and objects that are key-value pairs.[1] Objects created using the Object constructor, Object.create, or the literal object syntax (namely {}) are instances of Object. They can be thought of as an associative array, or dictionary objects. Objects are essentially a set of key-value pairs. If an object is asked to look up the value of a key, it will return the value associated with that key, or undefined if that key does not exist in the object.

Arrays on the other hand offer a sequential data structure, with efficient random lookup of elements. Arrays in JavaScripts are instances of the Array type, and they too are associative, except their keys are integers, and can only be integers that serve as the index of the item they point to.

Both objects and arrays give us ways to *reach into* them. Objects offer us the "dot" notation that allow us to fetch the value associated with a key within itself, as well as the "bracket" (or "subscript") notation (namely []) to the same effect. Arrays on the other hand offer only the bracket notation as a means to look up an element at a *particular* index within the array. Much like objects, looking up an index that does **not** exist within the array returns undefined.

Both objects and arrays can be nested, often one inside another. This can lead to rather convoluted lookups, forcing developers to inline variables to explain what they are trying to achieve. Observe:

```
const user = {
  name: 'douglas',
  profession: 'developer',
  address: {
    street1: '1 Ad Infinitum Drive',
    street2: ',
    city: 'Cupertino',
    state: 'CA',
    zip: [
```

---

[1]ES6 offers us two more data structures, namely Maps and Sets which we will see soon

```
      '95014',
      '1234',
    ],
  },
};
```

```
const zipCode = user.address.zip[0] + '-' + user.address.zip[1]; ①
console.assert(zipCode === '95014-1234');
```

```
// refactored version
const zip = user.address.zip; ②
const code = zip[0]; ③
const extended = zip[1];
const final = code + '-' + extended;
console.assert(final === '95014-1234');
```

> ① Use the obvious syntax
>
> ② Refactor it to make the intent clearer
>
> ③ What were to happen if the address object did **not** have a `zip` property?

Consider how we ascertained what the original object looks if we had not created it, but rather handed a reference to it. We would have to do some mental gymnastics to "rebuild" the structure of the original object by reverse parsing the lookup. This proves to be even more frustrating when functions expect an object or an array—as a client there is no way to tell which "parts" of the argument the function is really interested in without looking at its implementation or reading the docs.

To add salt to the wound, the syntax offers no provisions for `undefined` checks along the way! If an intermediate property fails the lookup, this failure cascades down to everything that relies on that property's value. Some languages offer a "safe navigation" operator, or a way to default a look up if it fails, but alas, we had no support for either in JavaScript.

The central tenet is the lack of symmetry between how we define objects and arrays (create the *structure*), and how we reach into them (*destructure* them) to get to particular values. If the lookup syntax mirrored the construction syntax, then "reassembling" the original object (or array) becomes trivial since the left-hand side of the assignment would be as expressive as the right-hand side.

Another aspect in the lack of destructuring support is the inability to spread or "splat" objects; in other words, get to **all** entries of a collection, be that elements of an array or key-value pairs in objects. Developers resort to imperatively iterating through whole collections, be that explicitly using for loops, or implicitly using methods like forEach, both of which leave much room for improvement.

Enter spread operator, and the new destructuring syntax. We will start with the spread operator, followed by the destructuring syntax.

# Spread Operator for Arrays

Consider a simple use-case—a function that calculates the perimeter of a triangle and an array that stores the lengths of the individual sides. Let us see how we would use the two together:

```
const perimeter = (a, b, c) => a + b + c;

const sides = [9, 8, 3]; ①

// prints 20
console.log(perimeter(sides[0], sides[1], sides[2])); ②
```

　　　　① We start with an array

　　　　② We extract every element of the array to supply to the function

Given that the function expects three arguments, we are forced to tease apart the values from the array using the subscript notation. This feels cumbersome. What would be nice is a way for us to "apply" the individual elements of the array as arguments to the function.

Well, now we can! We can now use the spread operator that expresses itself using the ... syntax. Observe how the same example morphs into the following:

```
const perimeter = (a, b, c) => a + b + c;

const sides = [9, 8, 3]; ①

// prints 20
console.log(perimeter(...sides)); ②
```

① We start with an array

② We use the spread operator to supply all the elements of the
array to the function

The spread operator syntax as demonstrated uses **...** as its syntactic construct.
It takes an array, and "explodes" it into its individual elements, passing each one as
individual arguments to the function. Right off the bat this eliminates our having to
extract the elements imperatively using the subscript syntax.

There are a handful of places in our code where we are allowed to use the spread
operator—first, as we have seen, is upon function invocation, and the second, array
construction, which we will see in the next section.

## "Expanding" Upon the Nuances of the Spread Operator

It will serve us best to first explore the spread operator in isolation. Consider our good
friend `console.log`. `log` is a multi-arity function, in that, given n arguments it writes
each value to the console delimited by whitespace. Let us simply use it to see the effects
of the spread operator:

```
const arr = [12, -3, 15, 44, 15, 36]; ①

// prints '[ 12, -3, 15, 44, 15, 36 ]'
console.log(arr); ②
// prints '12 -3 15 44 15 36'
console.log(...arr); ③

// to get the same result as we did with the spread operator
let temp = '';
for (const i in arr) {
  temp += arr[i];
  if (i != (arr.length - 1)) {
    temp += ' ';
  }
}
console.assert(temp === '12 -3 15 44 15 36'); ④
```

① We start with an array

② Simply print out the array—displays [ 12, -3, 15, 44, 15, 36 ]

③ Use the spread operator—displays 12 -3 15 44 15 36

④ Simulate what the spread operator does for us with `console.log`

As we might conclude, invoking `console.log` with an array *is* invoking it with **one** argument. However, invoking it with the spread operator acting on an array invokes with n arguments, where n is the length of the array.

The contrast is even more stark when we consider how we would have gone about printing *each* element of array to a space delimited string. Without the spread operator, we have no choice but to imperatively loop over the array, each time concatenating to a temporary string, which we would then pass to `console.log`.

The spread operator allows us to shift from an imperative mindset, where our intent is often lost amidst `for` loops and ceremony, to expressing our intent in a clear manner.

A pervasive use-case for the spread operator is one of concatenating arrays. Bear in mind that arrays have a `push` method available on them which adds items to the end of the array. Turns out `push` too is a multi-arity function. However, much like some of the `Math` operators, and `console.log`, this method is of little use if we wished to concatenate all the elements of one array to that of another.[2]

Another use-case for the spread operator is that of creating new arrays from existing ones. Let us study both these use-cases now:

```
const one = [12, -3, 15];
const otherOne = [...one]; ①
const two = [44, 15, 36]; ②

// mutation
one.push(...two); ③
console.log(one);

// alternatively inline the concatenation
const concatenated = [12, -3, 15, ...two]; ④
// prints '[ 12, -3, 15, 44, 15, 36 ]'
```

---

[2]We are back to imperatively taking each value out of the array, and then invoking `push` with each element one at a time.

```
console.log(concatenated);

// create a new array
const newArr = [...otherOne, ...two]; ⑤
// prints '[ 12, -3, 15, 44, 15, 36 ]'
console.log(newArr);
```

  ① Use the spread operator to copy an array into a new array

  ② We start with three arrays

  ③ push mutates the array in place

  ④ Create a *new* array concatenating elements, and an array

  ⑤ Create another array concatenating two arrays

We start with an array, and create a new one by exploding the first one inside the literal array notation ([]) of a new array. In other words, otherOne is a new array containing the same elements as our initial one.

The push method on Array, like console.log, happens to be a multi-arity method. So, we can easily push multiple elements from one array onto another, once again, using the spread operator. However, push performs a mutation, in that it changes the original array. However, functional programming encourages immutability, and if that is *our* intent, the spread operator is an ally.[3]

One nuance of the spread operator is that is does **not** perform a "flatten." If we spread an array of arrays, the end result will be the individual constituent arrays. The spread operator does not recursively explode the nested arrays.

The underlying machinery that makes the spread operator work relies on arrays being "iterable." We will cover iterables and iterators shortly; however it suffices to say that arrays abide by the iterator contract, thus enabling them to be used with the spread operator. Strings, Maps, and Sets (we will see those shortly as well) are also iterables, and thus can be spread.[4]

The biggest benefit of using the spread operator to construct new arrays is often the most overlooked one, in that, its syntax forces us to explode existing arrays into a new

---

[3]Libraries like Redux (https://redux.js.org/) urge us to adopt immutability for updates. Frameworks like Angular use a change detection strategy, and this can be further optimized by the use of immutable references.

[4]The utility of spreading a String is most certainly iffy; however it exists if you wish to use it.

array. We could achieve the same behavior by push-ing existing arrays onto an empty array, but that is not the intent of the push API. Rather, it is to mutate an existing array, which goes against the grain of functional programming.

## Spread vs. Rest—Polar Opposite Twins

One will have observed that the syntax for the rest parameter and the spread operator is identical, but their behavior is the exact opposite of one another. The rest parameter "collects" all the unaccounted arguments supplied to a function *into* an array, while the spread operator extracts all the elements *out* of an array. What differentiates what the ... syntax does depends on the invocation context. ... only acts as the rest parameter when an assignment happens, and if not, then it acts as a spread operator. This contradiction can be both interesting and disconcerting at the same time:

```
const onlyRest = (teacher, ...students) => {
  return [teacher, students.sort()]; ①
};

const restAndSpread = (teacher, ...students) => {
  return [teacher, ...students.sort()]; ②
};

// prints '[ 'Ada', [ 'Carol', 'Grace', 'Mary' ] ]'
console.log(onlyRest('Ada', 'Mary', 'Carol', 'Grace'));
// prints '[ 'Ada', 'Carol', 'Grace', 'Mary' ]'
console.log(restAndSpread('Ada', 'Mary', 'Carol', 'Grace'));
```

> ① Sort the rest arguments prior to appending the whole array in the return value
>
> ② Sort the rest arguments, and explode it to append its elements in the return value

We start by defining two multi-arity functions, both of which expect the name of the teacher, followed by n-number of names of students. Given that both functions declare a rest parameter, all arguments past the teacher are automatically bundled into an array. Both functions also proceed to sort the students' array prior to constructing the return value, which also happens be an array. However, it is here that the implementations depart from one another. In the case of the first function, we simply construct a new array with the name of the teacher, and the result of sort-ing the student array, which returns an array. The result as one might expect is an array of two elements—the name of the teacher followed by an array with the student names sorted.

However, in the second case, we *spread* the result of sort into the return value, thereby simply returning an array of strings, starting with the name of the teacher, followed by the names of the students sorted alphabetically. The difference between the two implementations is subtle; however the effect is profound.

We will see another place where the rest parameter is applicable, namely in array destructuring—but first, spreading objects.

# Spread Operator for Objects

Introduced in ES9, the ... operator is also available for "spreading" objects. Much like the ... operator we have seen for indexed collections, the ... operator "explodes" an object into its individual key-value pairs. However, before we get into the details of the spreading objects, we must talk about the characteristics of object properties, specifically the enumerable descriptor.

## Object.defineProperties

JavaScript developers are accustomed to constructing objects literally using the {} syntax, and tacking on arbitrary key-value pairs. These keys are by *default* enumerable, in that they will be listed if we were to use the for-in loop to iterate over the keys in the object.

Simultaneously, the Object class also provides us various (programmatic) mechanisms to create objects, as well as conveniences to configure them. One of these APIs is defineProperties which can be used along with a "descriptor" object to define functions and even getters/setters for existing objects.[5] The role of Object. defineProperties is to inject properties onto an existing object (hereon referred to as the "target") using the descriptor.

The descriptor acts as a placeholder to contain the configuration for each key that we wish to introduce onto the target. The descriptor object is a plain-old JavaScript object, whose keys will be installed on the target. Let's see how this is used with a simple example:

---

[5]There is also its cousin defineProperty that is useful if we are to only define one property at a time.

```
const michelle = {};
Object.defineProperties(michelle, { ①
  name: {
    value: 'Michelle', ②
  },
  hobby: {
    value: 'Gardening',
  },
});

// prints 'Michelle'
console.log(michelle.name);
// prints 'Gardening'
console.log(michelle.hobby);
```

① Invoke `defineProperties` with a target and descriptor object

② Define the `name` key with the `value` `Michelle`

The first argument is the object we wish to modify and the second argument happens to be the descriptor object, which as we can see is a JavaScript object with two keys. The value of every key in the descriptor object is the configuration for that property, and determines what form it will take in the target. That is, we are asking `defineProperties` to install two properties on the target object, namely `name` and `hobby`, with their associated values.

This aforementioned property, `value` is **not** arbitrary; it is a member of a select few that we are allowed to use as elucidated in `https://developer.mozilla.org/en-US/docs/Web/JavaScript/Reference/Global_Objects/Object/defineProperties`. These properties not only allow us to define a resultant property on the target as a value (remember, functions are values too in JavaScript), but also getter/setters and if the keys are `enumerable`, `writable`, and `configurable`.

Of these, `enumerable` is of particular interest to our soon-to-be-had discussion on `Object.assign`, so let us take a moment to explore its usage and meaning. Just like we set the `value` for a particular key using the descriptor object, and tack it on using `Object.defineProperties`, we can also supply it the `enumerable` setting. If the `enumerable` setting is **not** supplied alongside the `value` key in the descriptor object, its default is `false`. This is in stark contract with the default settings for keys installed in literal (`{}`)

object, which as we have discussed, happens to be `true`. This means that any property created using a descriptor object will **not** show up if were to iterate over the keys of the resultant object, unless we *explicitly* set the `enumerable` property to `true`:

```
const michelle = {};
Object.defineProperties(michelle, {
  name: {
    value: 'Michelle',
    enumerable: true, ①
  },
  hobby: {
    value: 'Gardening', ②
  },
});

for (const k in michelle) {
  if (Object.prototype.hasOwnProperty.call(michelle, k)) {
    // only prints 'name'
    console.log(k); ③
  }
}
```

① Set the enumerable key to true

② Since we are not setting `enumerable` here, it defaults to `false`

③ Only `name` shows up

The thing to note here is that any property that does **not** have the enumerable property set is *invisible* to the `for-in` loop. If we wanted to make all the keys visible, we could just as easily have used the literal object syntax to construct the object! That is to say, the role of `Object.defineProperties` is to allow us to *limit* how the world sees or affects the keys in our objects.

To return to the subject at hand, setting the enumerability of certain keys affects any algorithm that requires to interrogate an object for its keys, such as `JSON.stringify`, as well as the two new facilities that ES6 introduced, namely the newly added `Object.assign` as well as the object spread operator.

We will look at both `Object.assign`, introduced in ES6, and the spread operator for objects, introduced in ES9 in the following sections. At first glance they seem to do similar things, but as we will see, their intent is certainly different.

## Object.assign

ES6 gives us `Object.assign` as a means to copy all the enumerable keys of one object into another. `assign` takes a "target" object, followed by any number of "source" objects, and copies over all the *enumerable* keys of the source objects onto the target object. Consider the following example:

```
const michelle = { ①
  name: 'Michelle',
  hobby: 'Gardening',
};
const rachael = Object.assign({}, michelle, { ②
  name: 'Rachael',
  profession: 'Auditor',
});
// prints '{ name: 'Rachael', hobby: 'Gardening', profession: 'Auditor' }'
console.log(rachael);
```

① Initialize an object literally

② Use `Object.assign` to construct a new object that merges all the source objects

We start with creating an object literally with two keys. Recall that all such properties defined on an object are by default enumerable. We could have achieved the same effect if we had using `Object.defineProperties`, setting the `enumerable` descriptor for each of those keys to `true`.

Then we invoke `Object.assign` with a (blank) target, along with `michelle` and another (inlined) object literal. The thing to note here is that both `michelle` and the inline object have a property with the same name, which in case happens to be `name`. Therefore, if a single object were to copy over both (in order from left-to-right) then the last one wins. Right?

As the `console.log` demonstrates, the clone indeed has the union of the properties in the individual source objects. *However*, the name happens to be `Rachael,` which tells us that properties are indeed copied from left to right; in other words, both `michelle` and the inline object passed in as the sources have the same property, but it's the latter one that won.

One way to think about `Object.assign` is that is "explodes" the source objects into the target object, and if there happens to be a key collision, the last one wins. Furthermore, we can cleverly use this to create new objects from existing ones simply by targeting an empty object, as demonstrated.

Seemingly, `Object.assign` seems to do for objects what the spread operator does for iterables—it can help "spread" the key-value pairs of one object into another. However, it falls short on two accounts—the mechanisms to spread objects (`Object.assign`), and that for iterables (the spread operator) are not at par, in that they are syntactically different. Secondly, `Object.assign` is to objects what `Array.push` is to arrays, in that they both *mutate* the target object. Granted that we can supply an empty object as the target, however the intention of the API is to change the target.

`Object.assign` has a place in our toolkit; however, if we are to adopt a functional mindset and embrace immutability, then we need another ally. Allow me to introduce you to the spread operator for objects.

## Spreading Objects

ES9[6] brings the same operator that we use to spread iterables, namely ..., and makes them available for objects. This can be demonstrated by revisiting our earlier example:

```
const michelle = {
  name: 'Michelle',
  hobby: 'Gardening',
};
const rachael = {
  ...michelle, ①
  ...{
    name: 'Rachael',
```

---

[6]That is not a typo. Between ES6 and ES9 objects were not spread-able. The ability to spread objects landed 3 years later after it came in for iterables.

```
    profession: 'Auditor',
  },
};
```

```
// prints '{ name: 'Rachael', hobby: 'Gardening', profession: 'Auditor' }'
console.log(rachael);
```

       ① Use the spread operator

We start with a simple object, and attempt to construct a new object by spreading one or more objects into a new object. This example does not differ significantly from our earlier attempt except for the use of the spread operator instead of `Object.assign`. However, the new `...` syntax for objects does bring us to parity with how we spread iterables. Once again, the spread operator only copies over the enumerable properties of the object being spread.

Also note that the spread operator, just like `Object.assign`, respects the order in which we supply its sources. If two or more objects being spread happen to have the same key, the last key wins.

As we discussed in the previous section, the important distinction between `Object.assign` and the spread operator is the potential for side effects. `Object.assign` takes one target (as its first argument), followed by any number of sources. It then proceeds to *mutate* the target, copying the enumerable keys of sources into the target, and `return`-s the target object. If the target supplied happens to be an existing object, it is that object that will be endowed with the keys from the sources, thus changing that object.

On the flip side, the spread operator syntax offers us no such avenue. The very syntax of the spread operator forces us to spread existing objects into a *new* object. Putting it another way, the spread operator syntax encourages immutability.

# Destructuring

In an earlier discussion we deliberated upon the lack of symmetry between structuring (creation) and destructuring (reaching into) for arrays and objects. We touched upon several limitations of the existing approach, including the verbose syntax, the inability to default for "missing" parts, and lack of expressiveness in function signatures to advertise how they are to use their arguments. Now let us consider the new destructuring syntax, and how it addresses all of these concerns, followed by some of the caveats.

# Array Destructuring

The destructuring syntax for arrays reflects their sequential idiom. Observe.

```
const rgba = [239, 15, 255, 0.9]; ①
const [r, g, b, a, nonExistent] = rgba; ②
console.assert(r === 239);
console.assert(g === 15);
console.assert(b === 255);
console.assert(a === 0.9);
console.assert(nonExistent === undefined); ③

const [, , blue] = rgba; ④
const blueAgain = rgba[2];

console.assert(blue === b);
console.assert(blueAgain === b);
```

① We start with an array depicting the rgba value of the color pink

② We reach into the array using the destructuring syntax

③ Reaching for an element that the array does not have an index for returns undefined

④ If we wish to only reach a particular item in the array, we ignore other indexes

The destructuring syntax for arrays uses the [ ] syntax on the left hand, that is, assignment side of an expression. As we can see, the destructuring assignment permits us to assign variables in scope *positionally* just as we would define elements *for* an array. Now, the left-hand side of the assignment looks symmetric to the right-hand side. The syntax also allows us to skip indexes that may not be needed.

We can argue that the value of array destructuring when reaching for just one element is rather dubious when we could simply make use of the bracket notation, and it is a valid argument. However, the return of investment when interrogating for more than one element from an array certainly makes it worthwhile. Regardless, we can accede that operators like the bracket notation, or length still remain relevant, and should be used as and when deemed appropriate.

Furthermore, looking at the assignment we can attempt to *infer*[7] what the array on the right-hand side looks like.

Destructuring elements from an array does **not** violate the semantics that we are used to when working with the bracket notation. Just as asking an array for an element at an index that exceeds its `size` returns `undefined`, so does destructuring.

Consequently, any attempt to destruct `undefined` will result in an error. In fact, destructuring uses the same iterable machinery that the spread operator uses. Therefore, destructing *anything* that does not abide by the iterator interface (which we will see shortly) will result in an error.[8]

Much like default parameters, we can also default variable assignments in case an index of interest does not exist within the array like so:

```
const quadrilateral = [10, 15, 10, 15]; ①
const [q1 = 10,
       q2 = 20,
       q3 = q1,
       q4 = q2] = quadrilateral; ②

console.assert(q1 === 10);
console.assert(q2 === 15);
console.assert(q3 === 10);
console.assert(q4 === 15);

const [sq1 = 10,
       sq2 = sq1,
       sq3 = sq1,
       sq4 = sq1] = []; ③

console.assert(sq1 === 10);
console.assert(sq2 === 10);
console.assert(sq3 === 10);
console.assert(sq4 === 10);
```

---

[7]I must emphasize this. If we had an array with a thousand items in it, but only used destructuring to ask for the first three elements, all we can infer is the array is at least of length 3, and nothing more.

[8]Since maps and sets are iterables as we discussed before, these too can be destructured just like arrays, as we will see in a future chapter.

① Start with an array representing a quadrilateral

② Destructure with defaults assuming a rhombus

③ Destructure with defaults assuming a square

Just like default parameters in function arguments, not only can we default a variable if it does not exist in the originating array, but variables to the right can default to the values of previously extracted elements!

A function invocation in JavaScript also performs assignment; parameters in the method signature are assigned to each item in the argument list in turn. Turns out, we can destructure arrays directly in the method signature, along with defaulting them if they are not available in the array:

```
const perimeter = ([s1 = 10,
                     s2 = s1,
                     s3 = s1,
                     s4 = s2] = []) => { ①
  return s1 + s2 + s3 + s4;
};

console.assert(perimeter() === 40); ②
console.assert(perimeter([]) === 40); ③
console.assert(perimeter([15]) === 60); ④
console.assert(perimeter([15, 20]) === 70); ⑤
console.assert(perimeter([15, 20, 18, 23]) === 76); ⑥
```

① Default the whole array as well as each element in the array

② No argument invocation triggering the default

③ Effectively the same as above

④ Calculate the perimeter of a square

⑤ Calculate the perimeter of a rectangle

⑥ Calculate the perimeter of a trapezium

Everything we learned about default parameters applies here. We can default our parameters as a whole just like we would with the default parameter syntax, but if the parameter happens to be an array, we can destruct inline, as well as provide defaults to every element that we are interested in.

The clear upside is that the function signature is much more expressive, at the cost of being verbose. Formatting certainly helps here, and breaking down individual pieces of the parameters using new-lines is a well-adopted technique.

Finally, we can leverage the rest parameters as well with array destructuring.[9] This allows us to reach into an array to grab all the elements we are interested in, while simultaneously slurping the rest of the elements into another array.

```
const movies = ['Momento', 'Batman Begins', 'The Dark Knight'];

const [first, ...rest] = movies; ①
console.assert(first === 'Momento');
console.assert(Array.isArray(rest));

const [head, ...tail] = rest; ②
console.assert(head === 'Batman Begins');
console.assert(Array.isArray(tail));
```

① rest here is an array containing any unaccounted-for elements

② Recurse into the remaining elements

Like rest parameters for function signatures, usage of the rest pattern for destructuring **must** be the last assignment.

As we can see, this proves to be extremely useful in recursive algorithms[10]:

```
const or = (...args) => {
  if (args.length === 0) return null;
  if (args.length === 1) return args[0]; ①
  const [first, ...rest] = args; ②
  return first || or(...rest); ③
};

console.assert(or(null, undefined, true, false, '1'));
console.assert(!or(null, undefined, false));
```

---

[9]Reginald "Raganwald" Braithwaite has a brilliant article http://raganwald.com/2015/02/02/destructuring.html that explores destructuring and recursion.

[10]This is an instructive exercise in recursion; however, we must be careful when working in this paradigm with large arrays. If we are to work with large arrays, we might still have to consider imperatively operating over the array, thus eliminating any chance to blow the stack.

① Edge case detection

② Extract the elements we are interested in

③ Recurse if we need to

Finally, array destructuring can be used with nested arrays. Again, we can remark upon the symmetry between assignment and construction:

```
const ticTacToe = [
  ['x', 'o',  'x'],
  ['o', 'x', 'o'],
  ['x', 'o', 'x'],
];

const [
  [cell01] = [],
  [, cell11] = [],
  [, , cell22] = [], ①
] = ticTacToe; ②

console.assert(cell01 === 'x');
console.assert(cell11 === 'x');
console.assert(cell22 === 'x');
```

① Default an internal array look up in case the index lookup fails

② Nested destructuring

This example highlights a tripping hazard. If we are to recall our earlier discussion, looking up an index that an array does **not** possess results in an undefined. This may be acceptable if the value we seek is at the top level; however, this **will** result in an error if this is a nested lookup. Considering we are attempting to destruct undefined, this makes sense. The sanity check here might be to default the value of the entire (nested) lookup prior to destructuring it as demonstrated here.

One use-case for destructuring arrays is allow us to pretend that a function returns more than one value:

```
const distanceAndSlope = ([x1, y1], [x2, y2]) => {
  const distance = Math.hypot(x2 - x1, y2 - y1);
  const slope = (y2 - y1) / (x2 - x1);
```

```
  return [distance, slope]; ①
};
```

```
const [dist, slope] = distanceAndSlope([4, 3], [10, 12]); ②
```

```
console.assert(Number.parseFloat(dist.toFixed(2)) === 10.82);
console.assert(slope === 1.5);
```

① return an array (or a tuple in this case)

② Destructure to get multiple values out from the return

There are many methods in JavaScript that return an array (`RegExp.split` comes to mind), and array destructuring gives us a convenient and an eloquent way to use the result set of such functions.

Array destructuring is often used for destructing rest parameters. As we have seen, rest parameters capture all the "extra" arguments into an array, which is spreadable. This is particularly useful if we wish to treat the first element in the rest parameters arrays separately from the others. We often see this in recursive solutions, as seen here:

```
const flatten = ([first, ...rest]) => {
  if (first === undefined) return []; ①
  return !Array.isArray(first)
    ? [first, ...flatten(rest)]
    : [...flatten(first), ...flatten(rest)]; ②
};
```

```
const flattened = flatten([
  [1, 2],
  [3], 4, 5, [6, 7],
]);
```

```
console.assert(flattened.length === 7);
console.assert(flattened.join() === '1,2,3,4,5,6,7');
```

① Terminating case

② The essence of "flatten"-ing an array

We leverage the fact that if there are no rest parameters supplied, then destructuring will result in all elements being evaluated as undefined. That acts as the terminating case for recursion, else we continue with the recursion.

Aside from the clever use of destructuring and the spread operator, this example highlights how the new syntax introduced in ES6 allows us to approach functional programming idiomatically in JavaScript. Given a situation to flatten an array, our logical approach would be look at the first element in the array; if it happens to be an array itself, start by flattening that array, followed by flattening the remaining elements of the original array. This algorithm is revealed as-is in our approach. Without imperative loops, and unnecessary counters, our true intent is revealed in plain sight.

## Object Destructuring

The assignment operator, as one might expect, for objects is {}. Arrays are indexed by position; however, objects are key-value pairs. Consequently, the lookup mandates that we specify the *keys* we are interested in within the assignment. Observe:

```
const paip = {
  name: 'Paradigms of Artificial Intelligence Programming',
  author: 'Peter Norvig',
  isbn: 1558601910,
}; ①

const {
  name: n,
  isbn: id,
} = paip; ②

console.assert(n === 'Paradigms of Artificial Intelligence Programming');
console.assert(id === 1558601910);

const {
  name,
  isbn,
} = paip; ③

console.assert(name === 'Paradigms of Artificial Intelligence
Programming');
console.assert(isbn === 1558601910);
```

① We start with an object

② The long form of object destructuring

③ The short form of object destructuring

Object destructuring offers us two variants of the syntax. The longer version is useful when the variables we introduce in scope have names that do **not** line up with the keys in the object being destructured. The short form is useful if the names of the new variables are identical to the keys that they are interrogating.

Syntactically and semantically there is no sharp departure from that of array destructuring except that for objects we cannot positionally index, but rather we must specify the keys we are looking for.

Everything that is available to us in array destructuring is available to us here—undefined returns for nonexistent keys, default values, nested lookups, and destructuring support in method signatures are all up for grabs using object destructuring.

One aspect that is **not** available is the ability for new variables to see previously declared variables since "previous" implies an ordering, which does not exist for associative hashes.

Let us explore all of these facets:

```
const config = {
  size: 200,
  transitionMs: 750,
  clip: {
    width: 200,
  },
}; ①

const {
  size,
  transitionMs,
  clip: { ②
    width: w = 100, ③
    height = 100,
  } = {}, ④
} = config;
```

```
console.assert(size === 200);
console.assert(transitionMs === 750);
console.assert(w === 200);
console.assert(height === 100);

const drawChart = ({
  size = 200,
  transitionMs = 1000,
  clip: {
    width: w = 100,
    height = 100,
  } = {},
} = {}) => { ⑤
  return [size, transitionMs, w, height];
};

// invoke it
drawChart();
```

① We start with an object

② Using nested destructuring

③ Defaulted values using both long and short destructuring format

④ Default the entire nested lookup with a default in case the original object does not have the key

⑤ Destructuring in function parameters with defaults

Like arrays, objects return undefined if we attempt to look up a key that does not exist within the object. Once again, it is prudent to default a nested lookup in its entirety *prior* to looking up keys within it.

# Using Array and Object Destructuring in Combination

Of course, we can mix and match object and array destructuring. Let us revisit our earlier example to see how we can use a combination of the two to extract the parts we are interested in:

```
const user = {
  name: 'douglas',
  profession: 'developer',
  address: {
    street1: '1 Ad Infinitum Drive',
    street2: ",
    city: 'Cupertino',
    state: 'CA',
    zip: [
      '95014',
      '1234',
    ],
  },
};

const { ①
  address: { ②
    zip: [ ③
      zip, ④
      extended,
    ],
  },
} = user;

const final = zip + '-' + extended;
console.assert(final === '95014-1234');
```

① Destruct the outer object

② Since address is an object itself, we destruct that as well

③ zip happens to be an array

④ Reach for both indexes within zip simultaneously

Our intent is to extract the full zip code of the user, the elements of which happen to be inside an array, nested inside the `address` object, which in turn is a property inside a literal JavaScript object. Hence, we must exercise our nested destructuring skills, carefully peeling apart the original structure to surgically retrieve exactly what it is that we want. We start by destructuring the outer object, which in turn leads us to the `address` key, which we must destruct again to fetch the `zip` array. Finally, we can use the array destructuring syntax to fetch the elements that constitute the zip code by index. Phew!

We have come full circle. Gone are the convoluted lookups and the unnecessary variables. What remains is simply what we seek. And once again, the symmetry between structuring and destructuring is revealed.

# Caveats

There remains one final limitation that is specific to destructuring in function signatures. It just so happens that if we destructure an argument supplied to a function, we lose the reference to the whole object (or array). In other words, we have a choice—we either destructure to get the parts we need or we grab the whole object and destructure within the implementation of the function allowing us to use the whole object further on. While this may sound like an edge-case, there are times when we need to use parts of an object, and then send the whole object downstream for further processing. Languages like Clojure offer the use of the `:as` keyword as a means to destruct and hold a reference to the whole object. Unfortunately, JavaScript offers us no such recourse.

# A Small Distinction

The spread and rest operator that works for iterables is different than the one that applies to objects in that objects are **not** iterable! While the spread and rest operator look and behave the same for both iterables and objects, the underlying mechanisms used for the two are very different. We should treat the spread and rest operator that works for objects as *new* syntax vs. treating it as an extension of the operators we work for iterables.

This disparity also reveals itself when we attempt to use the spread operator in conjunction with multi-arity functions like `console.log`. Recall that if we have an iterable (like an array) and wish to supply the contents of the array to `console.log`, we can simply invoke it using `console.log(...arr)`. This will "explode" the array, supplying the items of the array as individual arguments to `log`. This will not work for objects, once again a gentle reminder that objects are not iterable, and do not lend themselves to all of the use-cases that work for iterables.

# Summary

The spread operator as we have seen provides us with a very powerful mechanism to get at *all* the elements of an array in one fell swoop. This proves particularly useful when working with multi-arity functions, as well as when creating and/or concatenating arrays from other arrays.

The destructuring syntax on the other hand provides us a means to interrogate data using a *domain-specific language* (DSL) that resembles the syntax that we use to create objects in the first place. Consequently, this DSL proves to be just as expressive, and with additional functionality such as defaulting missing properties (and indexes), this is yet another useful tool in our JavaScript toolkit.

In the next chapter, we will shift directions, and look at a new mechanism to define strings that helps simplify creating both dynamic and multiline strings.

# CHAPTER 5

# Formatted Strings Using Template Strings

## Introduction

Ever tried to create a dynamic string in JavaScript that involved interpolating more than one variable at a time? I always seem to mess up the + and the quotes somehow. And heaven forbid we must format it in a particular way with new-lines and indentation. Also, let's not talk about *ever* changing that once we get it written out, shall we?

In this chapter we will forever forgo string concatenation in lieu of template strings which allow us to lay out strings that interpolate variables and expressions in a clear and declarative manner. We will also explore tag functions, which can be used to create DSLs in JavaScript. I assure you that by the end of this chapter, you will be itching to refactor every string in your codebase to use template strings. You might even walk away with some ideas on how you can whip up your own DSL!

© Raju Gandhi 2019
R. Gandhi, *JavaScript Next*, https://doi.org/10.1007/978-1-4842-5394-6_5

# The Trouble with Forming Formed Strings

JavaScript has the String primitive, and supports constructing strings literally using single quotes or double quotes.[1] However, while this works for constructing strings that are static, they prove to be rather cumbersome to work with when building strings programmatically. Consider the following:

```
const salutation = 'Mr.';
const name = 'Edgar';
const middle = 'Allen';
const last = 'Poe';
const fullName = (salutation ? salutation + ' ' : '') ①
                 + name + ' ' + middle.trim() + ' ' + last; ②
// prints 'Mr. Edgar Allen Poe'
console.log(fullName);
```

    ① Ensure we need to put in a salutation if provided

    ② Compose the full name ensuring no middle name if there isn't one

As we can see, the intent of what it is we are trying to accomplish is lost as we attempt to distinguish between the "static," or fixed pieces of the string, and the "dynamic," or variable pieces of the string. This problem, of course, is further accentuated if the dynamic pieces happen to contain function or method calls, conditionals, or looping constructs.

Many modern JavaScript (and single-page application) frameworks like Angular allow us to embed HTML in the same files as JavaScript (or TypeScript). HTML, like our JavaScript code, is best written and more importantly maintained if it is formatted correctly.

---

[1]Idiomatically the JavaScript community has leaned toward using single quotes, leaving double quotes for usage scenarios like writing JSON, and situations where we might write HTML in JavaScript. This pattern has found itself codified in popular linters, such as Airbnb's (https://github.com/airbnb/javascript/blob/96317f8c79d6c5a6e9478a49eb89770863c4e6e1/README.md#strings%E2%80%94%E2%80%8Bquotes).

Given that our only available option is string concatenation, we are forced to participate in interpolation and indentation machinations[2]:

```
const title = 'Section Title'; ①
function HelloComponent() { };
HelloComponent.annotations = [new ng.core.Component({
  selector: 'app-hello-world',
  template: '<article class="content">' + ②
              '<section class="section">' +
                '<div class="col-md-12">' +
                  '<div class="card">' +
                    '<div class="card-block">' +
                      '<div class="card-title-block">' +
                        '<h3 class="title">' + title + '</h3>' + ③
                      '</div>' +
                    '</div>' +
                  '</div>' +
                '</div>' +
              '</section>' +
            '</article>'
})];
```

① Declare a variable

② Attempt to construct a rather elaborate string using string concatenation

③ Use the variable inline

Good programmers do not let their friends review badly formatted code. Thus, we are not only forced to break up lines using the + operator, we also need to ensure that our code is correctly indented. However, in this case, our editor assumes this to be JavaScript, not realizing that it is actually HTML embedded *in* JavaScript and will

---

[2]Angular 6+ strongly enforces the use of TypeScript as the lingua franca. TypeScript is a super-set of JavaScript and supports everything we speak of in this book. However, this example reveals how one would write a component for Angular using plain old ES5 JavaScript. Although this practice is now discouraged, the essence of the problem remains untarnished, thus serving as a good illustration of the limitations of JavaScript strings.

proceed to re-indent all of the code if asked to do so (if it does not do it automatically!). Of course, this concern extends itself to almost any embedded DSL, wherein we have a conflation of interpolated variables, and formatting.

Given what we have, we resort to string concatenation, an archaic interpolation mechanism, all while painstakingly hitting the Enter key at appropriate line lengths in the hope that our linting tool will not fail our build because we left one too many lines badly formatted.

Well, our worries are over. ES6 introduces template literals, and as an extension, tagged template literals.

# Template literals

Template literals introduce more syntax, namely the back-tick, or ` as a mechanism to declare strings, and additionally, placeholder syntax, namely ${}, to support interpolation of variables and expressions. Template literals make it easier to compose strings consisting of both literal strings and expressions in-line that are to be evaluated as part of the string creation. Consider the following:

```
const greeting = 'Hola'; ①
const name = 'Daniel';

const msg = `${greeting}! My name is ${name}`; ②
```

> ① Introduce some constant placeholders
>
> ② Compose a string using a template literal with variable interpolation

The template literal *literally* lays out a string, minus the hoops one has to jump through with meticulously placed + operators. Appropriately named variables used in interpolation within the ${} can aid in furthering readability.

The interpolation syntax accepts any expression—be that function calls, math operations, or even ternary expressions.[3]

---

[3]Recall that an expression always evaluates to *something*. Statements, such as if conditions, for/while loops, and switch-case, on the other hand, do not evaluate to anything, and thus do not qualify to be used in template literals.

Template literals can also be used to lay out multiline strings. If used in this manner, they retain the layout upon evaluation. Given that many modern editors and IDEs already support ES6 syntax, having them auto-format your code means that we no longer lose our layout. Let us see how this were to look if we were to revisit our Angular component example:

```
const title = 'Section Title'; ①
function HelloComponent() { };
HelloComponent.annotations = [new ng.core.Component({
  selector: 'app-hello-world',
  template: `
    <article class="content"> ②
      <section class="section">
        <div class="col-md-12">
          <div class="card">
            <div class="card-block">
              <div class="card-title-block">
                <h3 class="title">${title}</h3> ③
              </div>
            </div>
          </div>
        </div>
      </section>
    </article>`
})];
```

① Declare a variable

② Use a template literal to compose a string

③ Interpolate a variable inline

Template literals retain **all** the formatting we introduce within the back-ticks. In our example our string starts with a newline character, with every line following it indented with two spaces. If we were to simply print it out using `console.log`, we will see that the template literal remains true to its word. Again, aided by the fact that most editors now support ES6 syntax, it is easy to spot where we are laying out strings literally, as opposed to where we are using the interpolation syntax.

There is one limitation of the interpolation syntax, and that is, we cannot nest interpolations. Let us look at an example:

```
// for illustrative purposes _ marks a whitespace
{
  const name = 'Edgar';
  const middle = 'Allen';
  const last = 'Poe';
  // prints 'Edgar_Allen_Poe'
  console.log(`${name} ${middle} ${last}`); ①
}

{
  const name = 'Emily';
  const middle = '';
  const last = 'Dickinson';
  // prints 'Emily__Dickinson'
  console.log(`${name} ${middle} ${last}`);
  // prints 'Emily__Dickinson' ②
  console.log(`${name} ${middle.trim()} ${last}`);
  // console.log(`${${name} ${middle}}.trim() ${last}`); ③
  // prints Emily_Dickinson
  console.log(`${`${name} ${middle}`.trim()} ${last}`); ④
}
```

① Works in an ideal case

② Oops! One too many whitespaces

③ Attempting to nest interpolations will not work

④ We can take advantage of the fact that template literals evaluate to strings

In our ideal case, every candidate has a first, middle, and last name. However, in the case where we do not have a middle name, blindly concatenating strings without a `trim` in the right places results in one too many spaces. Also, note that our attempt to `trim` the middle name is also misplaced—trimming the middle name aids in reducing redundant whitespace if the name itself consisted of trailing whitespace. However, it does nothing for the space *around* an empty middle name.

What we would like to do is concatenate the first and middle name, `trim` to eliminate any redundant whitespace, and only then tack on the last name.

Since we cannot nest interpolations, we are forced to take a different tack. We can leverage the fact that template literals evaluate to their resultant strings—thus we can nest template strings within template strings—and in a slightly convoluted way, nest interpolations.

While one might object to the readability of nested template strings, and that objection is well justified, it is not uncommon to see it, especially in light of tagged literals, as we will see soon.

Another limitation is the interpolation syntax *is* ${}, in that, the $ and the {} are required. Many languages like Ruby allow you to skip the {} if simply evaluating a variable, whereas mandate them when evaluating any expression.

What if we wanted to have a back-tick, or a $ sign as a literal? Simple enough. Just escape them using a backslash, as shown here:

```
const escapingLiterals = `Template strings introduce \`\` and use $\{} for
interpolation`;
// prints 'Template strings introduce `` and use ${} for interpolation'
console.log(escapingLiterals);
```

Template literals solve the problem of composing strings quite elegantly—allowing us to express how a string is to be formed and formatted succinctly. But there is even more good news! ES6 affords us yet another facility that works with template strings, namely tagged literals. Let us look into these next.

# Tagged Literals

Tagged literals allow us to use "tags," or tag functions, in conjunction with template literals, so that we can affect the resulting string and produce more than what we might be able to accomplish with template literals alone.

Let us take a step back and see how template literals work. There are two aspects of a template literal that we can use to change the resultant string—*how* we concatenate and what we can do with the variables that we interpolate within the template. Consider a situation in which we interpolate string variables within a template string—the manner in which we affect the result depends on what the string object is capable of.

For example, we could invoke the `toUpperCase` method and have a rather effervescent message displayed, like so:

```
const greeting = 'Hello';
const name = 'Sylvia';
const msg = `${greeting.toUpperCase()}! My name is ${name}!`;
```

If we were to tease apart the constituent parts of a template string, we see that there are two parts to the equation—the "static" pieces of the string and the "dynamic" pieces of the string. We can envision these as two arrays, like so:

*Static vs. dynamic pieces of template strings*

```
const greeting = 'Hello';
const name = 'Sylvia';
const msg = `${greeting}! My name is ${name}!`; ①
//                 _____-------------_____- ②

const fixedStrings = ["", '! My name is ', '!']; ③
const values = ['Hello', ' Sylvia']; ④
```

  ① A template string interpolating just two variables

  ② - denote fixed parts, _ represent dynamic parts

  ③ The parts of the string that are fixed represented as an array

  ④ The dynamic, or evaluated pieces of the template string

Just like we did here, we can take *any* template string, and splice it neatly into two arrays. Furthermore, if we interleaved these two arrays—taking the first item from the `fixedStrings` array, concatenating it with the first value from the `values` array, and proceeding till we run out of items—we can reconstitute the template strings ourselves!

Tag functions allow us to do exactly this. They let us intercept the evaluation of the template string by giving us a reference to the constituent parts of the template—the fixed and dynamic pieces, and whatever the return value of the tag function happens to be, is neatly slotted in where we invoked it.

We will start with a simple example, in which we will implement the functionality offered to us by template strings themselves. This will give us an opportunity to understand how to use tag functions, and inspect their signature:

```
const handler = (strings, ...values) => {  ①
  const interleave = (arr1, arr2) =>
    arr1.reduce((arr, v, i) => arr.concat(v, arr2[i]), []);
  return interleave(strings, values).join(");
};

const greeting = 'Hello';
const name = 'Ernest';

const msg = handler`${greeting}! My name is ${name}.`;  ②
// prints 'Hello! My name is Ernest.'
console.log(msg);
```

①  Declare a tag function

②  Invoke the tag function, handing it a template string

Tag functions have a unique invocation pattern, in that, unlike regular functions that must wrap their arguments in parenthesis, tag functions simply accept a template string in-line. JavaScript splits the template string into its fixed and dynamic parts, passing them into the tag function separately—all of the fixed parts are sent in as the first argument as an array, with the interpolated values sent in consecutively in the same order as they appear in the original template. Thus, in our example, `strings` is an array of the fixed parts, and we simply capture all of the remaining arguments into an array using the variable arguments syntax.

The rest is simple—simply interleave the two arrays, starting with the first item of the `strings` array, followed by one from the `values` array, and proceed till we reach the end of the `strings` array, and return the result.

If you were to try this out in the console, you will see that you can supply it any template string, and it will return the string just as if were evaluated by JavaScript.

So far, we have implemented something that JavaScript already does for us, so perhaps you are not convinced why tag functions are a good idea. Let us attempt a slightly more elaborate example—there is a very popular extension for many editors called Emmet.[4] Once installed, it allows one to write HTML (and CSS) incredibly fast by providing a highly abbreviated syntax that unfolds into valid HTML code. Emmet goes one step further, placing the cursor in the right position after expansion, allowing us the

---

[4]https://emmet.io/

type in the inner HTML. Consider the following examples, where the comments express what a developer would type in their editor that supports Emmet, followed by the Tab key, to see what Emmet would convert the text into (with the _ revealing where the cursor would be placed by Emmet):

```
<!-- h3.title -> TAB -->
<h3 class="title">_</h3>
<!-- h3.title.content -> TAB -->
<h3 class="title content">_</h3>
<!-- h3.title.content#main -> TAB -->
<h3 class="title content" id="main"></h3>
```

Emmet syntax is obviously inspired by CSS selectors, such as those that are accepted by document.querySelector and jQuery. Emmet is an interactive medium, in that it can place the cursor at the appropriate spot for the developer to type in the text that represent the innerHTML for the element.

What if we wanted to do something similar programmatically, wherein we could supply Emmet inspired syntax, and our code would expand it into the appropriate HTML? Of course, we need a way to express the innerHTML of the element, since we are going to actually write out all the HTML and don't have the luxury of appropriately placing a cursor, so we are going to pull a fast one. We will use template literals and tag functions, with one restriction—the innerHTML to the element has to be supplied as an interpolated variable at the end of the template string. In other words, h1.title${someVar} is valid, but h1.title.content${someVar}#main is not. This will let us know which parts compose the HTML element, and what text to place in as the innerHTML.

Finally, given h1.title${someVar} where someVar evaluates to some text the tag function should return <h1 class="title">some text</h1>. Ready?

```
function ele([strings], ...values) { ①
  const str = strings.trim();
  // assume anything before the FIRST . or # to be the name of the element
  const [element] = str.split(/[.#]/); ②

  // split the remainder of the string into parts using . or # as the
     delimiter
  // this will grab everything between a '.' or '#' and the next '.' or '#'
```

```
  const attrs = str.match(/[.#](?:[^.#]+)/g); ③

let idStr = '';
let classStr = '';
if (attrs) { ④
  // find all ids supplied
  // if multiple ids were supplied just use the last one
  const id = attrs
    .filter(a => a.startsWith('#'))
    .pop(); ⑤
  // do not compose id string if no ids were supplied
  idStr = id
    ? `id="${id.substring(1, id.length)}"` ⑥
    : '';

  // find all classes supplied
  const classes = attrs
    .filter(a => a.startsWith('.'))
    .map(v => v.substring(1, v.length)); ⑦
  // do not compose class string if no classes were supplied
  classStr = (classes.length > 0)
    ? `class="${classes.reduce((acc, v) => `${acc}${v} `, '').trim()}"` ⑧
    : '';
}

const adornedElement = [element, idStr, classStr]
  .reduce((acc, v) => `${acc} ${v}`.trim(), ''); ⑨
return `<${adornedElement}>${values.join('')}</${element}>`; ⑩
}

const heading = 'Hello Template Handlers';

// prints '<h1>Hello Template Handlers</h1>'
console.log(ele`h1 ${heading}`);
// prints '<h1 id="main">Hello Template Handlers</h1>'
console.log(ele`h1#main ${heading}`);
// prints '<h1 class="title">Hello Template Handlers</h1>'
console.log(ele`h1.title ${heading}`);
```

```
// prints '<h1 id="main" class="title content">Hello Template Handlers</h1>'
console.log(ele`h1.title.content#main ${heading}`);
// prints '<h1 id="main" class="title content"><div>Hello Template
Handlers</div></h1>'
console.log(ele`h1.title.content#main ${ele`div${heading}`}`);
// prints '<h1 id="main" class="title content"><div class="banner">Hello
Template Handlers</div></h1>'
console.log(ele`h1.title.content#main ${ele`div.banner${heading}`}`);
```

① Our Emmet compliant tag function

② Assume the name of the element to be the first thing in the supplied string

③ Use a regular expression to get all class/Ids markers

④ Nothing to do if it just a plain element with no attributes

⑤ Get the `id`, and if multiple ids were supplied, take the last one

⑥ Build the `id=""` string

⑦ Filter for all attributes starting with `.`

⑧ Build the `class=""` string

⑨ Build the opening tag string with id/class specified

⑩ Write out the full element including its `innerHTML` and return it

There is a lot going on here, so let us take it one step at a time. Given the constraints we have placed on the usage of our tag functions, we know that the array containing the element description will be a single element array. Hence, we destructure the same to get that one and only element and `trim` it to eliminate any superfluous whitespace. We also know that the string consists of an element name followed by class (`.`) and id (`#`) selectors, so we can use `split` to get anything before the first appearance of a selector and treat that as the name of the HTML element we are to produce.

Next, some regular expression magic to grab every selector that was supplied after the element name into an array. So, if the user were to supply `h1.title.content#main` then the regular expression would split this into an array that looks like `['.title', '.content', '#main']`. We first filter this array to find all the IDs supplied by the user, and if there were more than one (which is illegal), we simply take the last one supplied, thereby emulating the behavior of Emmet, and compose the `id=` string. However, multiple classes *are* allowed, so we filter our array for all the supplied classes and compose the `class=` string.

The rest is easy—simply bring together the name of the element, the id, and class string, ensuring we are interjecting the `innerHTML` content (supplied as interpolated variables), and return the fully composed element.

We must highlight a few things about our implementation. First, we use template strings *within* our function to construct other strings. In so far as a tag function is concerned, other than having an explicit signature, they are just like regular functions. Secondly, as we can see in the examples, we can nest other (tag) function invocations, allowing us to create nested element structures. Since JavaScript has to first evaluate every interpolated expression prior to composing the string, in effect, nested calls to our tag function cause the final string to be built inside out—with the innermost invocation happening first, then moving outward.

Admittedly our implementation is not going to win any awards any time soon. It cannot handle sibling elements (which Emmet supports with the + operator) or creating n number of elements simultaneously (Emmet does this with the ∗ operator). However, it does allow us to get some insight into the power of template literals and tag functions, and what they are truly capable of.

Tag functions, along with template strings offer a variety of use-cases, including aiding with internationalization and localization, language translation, and sanitation of user input, where the core essence is transforming a string from one form into another. We could even extend our emmet tag function to emulate behavior exhibited by template languages like JSX[5] from React. Libraries like styled-component[6] and html-tagged-template[7] offer great ideas and incentives for us to consider template literals for many common day-to-day use-cases.

Can you think of any situation where you can eliminate redundancy in your code by introducing such a DSL? How about times where you might be pretty-printing objects for debugging purposes? Or displaying data in a particular format, like locale-specific dates and/or currencies?

---

[5]https://reactjs.org/docs/introducing-jsx.html
[6]https://github.com/styled-components/styled-components
[7]https://github.com/straker/html-tagged-template

# Summary

Generating strings that interpolate variables has always been a tedious affair, and template strings aim to alleviate the pain by providing a literal that not only makes it easier, but also has support for multiline strings. Tag functions, on the other hand, allow us to intercept how construction of template strings, allowing for some rather interesting use-cases.

In the next chapter we will switch our attention back to objects and arrays. Objects and arrays have served us well so far, but those of us who come from other languages, we often reminisce about data-structures such as maps and sets, and the lack of such data-structures in JavaScript. That is to be the topic of our next chapter. Alongside we will see how the spread operator and destructuring work hand in hand with these as well.

# CHAPTER 6

# Maps and Sets—The New Data-structures on the Block

A programming language must provide us with all of the necessary constructs that empower developers to model their domain and problem space clearly and efficiently. Till date, JavaScript lacked support for two fundamental types that most other languages offer, namely maps and sets. This changes in ES6.

In this chapter we will explore the use-cases for two new data-structures introduced in ES6, namely Maps and Sets. We will start with their construction and understand their API, and even take a look under the hood to see how they are implemented. By the end of this chapter, we will have a complete understanding of how and when we can leverage maps and sets in our code, and when it is best to avoid them.

## Why Objects are Not Enough

JavaScript offers us two "collection"-like objects—objects (represented via the { } literal) and arrays (represented using the [ ] literal). Objects, often referred to as associative arrays, or dictionaries provide lookup via keys. Arrays on the other hand provide a sequential data-structure that provide efficient random lookup via indexes.

© Raju Gandhi 2019
R. Gandhi, *JavaScript Next*, https://doi.org/10.1007/978-1-4842-5394-6_6

Objects and arrays, while useful, do not prove to be sufficient for all use-cases. One limitation of objects serving as a *true* key-value store is that object keys **are** strings. In other words, the "type" of the key is not retained when used in an object. This can be trivially demonstrated:

```
const obj1 = {
  'true': 'String',
  true: 'Boolean',
}; ①

console.assert(obj1[true] === 'Boolean'); ②

const obj2 = {
  true: 'Boolean',
  'true': 'String',
}; ③

console.assert(obj2[true] === 'String'); ④
```

① Create an object with two *seemingly* different keys

② Interrogate the object for a key with a type

③ Swap the order of key value pairs with **no other change**

④ The same lookup is now different

This is patently clear to anyone (which is *all* of us) who has ever serialized a JavaScript object to JSON.

Given this limitation, if we needed to retain the *type* of the key we had no recourse.[1]

ES6 in response offers us maps and sets. Maps, much like objects, are key-value stores; however, they retain the types of their keys, proving to be closer to maps offered in other languages. Sets on the other hand fill in a role that prior to ES6 had developers resorting to lots of === checks against entries in arrays, resigning to using only strings as "unique entries" in objects, or if all failed, reaching out for third-party libraries[2] to fulfill their needs.

Our quest ends here. We start by exploring maps, followed by sets.

---

[1]Arrays too store their indexes as strings.

[2]http://code.google.com/p/jshashtable

# Maps

Maps, much like objects, present a lookup via a key, with the difference being that maps retain the *type* of the key (vs. coercing them into strings like objects do). Maps offer us a constructor as a means to create new maps. Unlike arrays and objects, they do **not** offer us a literal for construction, which has an implication on their serializability (which we will see soon). Maps also offer us a comprehensive API to add, update, and delete key-value pairs within the map, all of which are demonstrated here:

*Map key-value API*

```
const obj = {};
const map = new Map(); ①

map.set('string', 'is a string'); ②
map.set(true, 'is a boolean');

map.set(1, 'is a number').set(obj, 'is an object'); ③

console.assert(map.has(1)); ④
console.assert(map.get(obj) === 'is an object'); ⑤

map.set(1, 'overrides first'); ⑥
console.assert(map.get(1) === 'overrides first'); ⑦

console.assert(map.delete('string')); ⑧
console.assert(map.has('string') === false);

console.assert(map.delete({}) === false); ⑨
```

① Constructor to create a map

② set a key

③ set is a fluent API returning the map itself

④ has implies possession

⑤ get is the interrogation API

⑥ Forcing a collision causes the previous *value* to be overwritten

⑦ Last one wins

⑧ If an existing key is deleted then the map returns true

⑨ Deletion of a nonexistent key

The Map API provides us with all we need to work with keys and values. The set API being fluent certainly proves to be a worthy ally, allowing to avoid some of the verbosity that results if that were not the case. Collisions are handled as we might expect, and finally, we can use the delete API to remove a key-value pair from the map, which returns true if the key was indeed deleted from the map (delete will return a false if the key did not exist, thereby having nothing to delete).

At a higher level there are APIs that let us work with the map as a whole, allowing us to get all entries, the count of entries, even clear the map if we wish to do so:

```
const map = new Map([ ①
  ['s', 'is a string'], ②
  [true, 'is a boolean', 'willBeIgnored'], ③
  [1], ④
  [], ⑤
]);

console.assert(map.size === 4); ⑥

console.assert(map.get('s') === 'is a string');
console.assert(map.get(true) === 'is a boolean');
console.assert(map.get(1) === undefined);

console.assert(map.get(undefined) === undefined);
console.assert(map.has(undefined));

map.forEach((v, k) => console.log(v, k)); ⑦

console.log(map.entries());
console.log(map.keys());
console.log(map.values()); ⑧
map.clear(); ⑨
console.assert(map.size === 0);
```

① Alternative constructor taking an iterable

② Tuple representing key-value pairs

③ Extra elements in tuples are discarded

④ Only key, so value is set to undefined

⑤ Both key-value pairs are missing

⑥ Slightly discombobulating property to interrogate for count

⑦ Functional API to iterate over key-value pairs

⑧ All of these return iterators

⑨ An API to clear the map and set its `size` to zero

Maps offer another helpful constructor that can use any "iterable" to create maps out of. A common idiom is to supply the constructor with an array of arrays. Each nested array is assumed to be a two-value tuple, representing key and value. If the nested array contains only one item, then the value is set to `undefined`. If the array contains more than two items, then all extra elements are ignored. Finally, if the array is empty then both key and value are set to `undefined`. If the supplied array produces **no** collisions, then the resulting map will have its keys ordered in the same manner as the array, and the `size` of the resulting map will be equal to the `length` of the array.

Interestingly maps retain the insertion order of their entries, specifically the order in which the **keys** were added. However, if there happens to be a collision, then the new value overrides the previous value *at the location where the key exists*. That is, they act very much like arrays except their "indexes" happen to be of any type.

Since maps maintain order, they allow us to iterate over their `entries` with methods like `forEach`, as well as the `entries` API which returns one key-value pair at a time, wrapped in an array of `length` 2 represented as `[key, value]`. Maps also expose a `keys` and a `values` API, which, as their names suggest, return an array of the keys and values in the map, in insertion order.

Maps, like arrays abide by the "iterator" contract, which as we have discussed earlier, allows maps to be spreadable using the … operator, and consequently be destructured. Maps as we have seen can be created using an array of arrays; conversely spreading a map, as one might deduce, explodes a map into an array of arrays, with each array being a tuple of key and value, and the encompassing array reflecting the order of insertion, and its `length` being the `size` of the map.

```
const firstQuarter = new Map([
  [1, 'Jan'],
  [2, 'Feb'],
  [3, 'Mar'],
  [4, 'Apr'],
]); ①
```

```
const mapToStr = [...firstQuarter].join(':'); ②
console.assert(mapToStr === '1,Jan:2,Feb:3,Mar:4,Apr');

const [

  ,
  [n2, m2],
  [n3, m3],
] = firstQuarter; ③

console.assert(n2 === 2);
console.assert(m2 === 'Feb');
console.assert(n3 === 3);
console.assert(m3 === 'Mar');
```

① Create a map

② Explode a map into an array

③ Destruct for the second and third entries

Given that maps are iterable, and that the Map constructor expects an iterable, proves to be very convenient when we attempt to create new maps from existing maps. This is even handier when creating new maps that happen to be the union of other maps:

```
const nihar = new Map([
  ['car', 'mazda'],
  ['residence', 'apartment'],
]);

const ericka = new Map([
  ['pet', 'oscar'],
  ['residence', 'house'],
]);

const union = new Map([...nihar, ...ericka]); ①

console.assert(union.get('car') === 'mazda');
console.assert(union.get('residence') === 'house'); ②
console.assert(union.get('pet') === 'oscar');
```

① Union of two maps

② "last one in" mantra

We start with two separate maps, and then attempt to construct a new one by leveraging the fact that maps are "spreadable", and that the map constructor can utilize an array to construct a new map. Notice that in this case, the array that is passed to the constructor has **four** entries; however, as the map attempts to add each entry to the new map, it detects a collision when encountering the `residence` key. Thus, the resulting array will have `house` as the value for the `residence` key.

To round out maps, let us answer the pertinent question that still remains to be answered—what deems two keys to be the same? The answer lies in the === operator. If upon a `set` any existing key in the map returns `true` for a === test against any of its keys, that is deemed a collision, and the value for that key will be set to the new value. Otherwise, a new key-value entry is inserted at the end of the map.

# Caveats

There aren't too many caveats associated with maps. The API is comprehensive and does all we expect a map to do.

However, the first strike is the lack of a literal. This forces us to use the constructor, and seems to be against the grain of how we usually work with objects and arrays. There are many reasons not to use constructors in JavaScript[3] but alas, no recourse for us here. Let us observe this dichotomy with a simple example:

```
const kiran = { ①
  name: 'kiran',
  profession: 'pharmacist',
};

const favFruits = [ ②
  'mango',
  'guava',
  'pineapple',
];
```

---

[3]JavaScript Patterns by Stoyan Stefanov [O'Reilly, 2010].

```
const numbersInHindi = new Map(); ③
numbersInHindi.set(1, 'ek').set(2, 'do').set(3, 'teen');
```

① Objects offer us the literal { } syntax

② Similarly arrays offer us the [ ] literal

③ We are forced to use the constructor

The second concern involves serializing (and deserializing) to (and from) JSON. The JSON specification[4] accommodates only two data-structures—objects and arrays. Consequently, using JSON.stringify on any map does not do what one would expect.

Turns out, the closest we can get to a serialized version of a map is to treat it as an array of arrays. On the other end, we can simply JSON.parse the string we receive, and hand it to the map constructor to create a new map out of it. Observe:

```
const nihar = new Map([
  ['car', 'mazda'],
  ['residence', 'apartment'],
]);
```

```
const mapToJson = map => JSON.stringify([...map]); ①
const jsonToMap = mapStr => new Map(JSON.parse(mapStr)); ②
```

```
const serialized = mapToJson(nihar);
// prints '[["car","mazda"],["residence","apartment"]]'
console.log(serialized);
```

```
const deserialized = jsonToMap(serialized);
// prints 'Map { 'car' => 'mazda', 'residence' => 'apartment' }'
console.log(deserialized);
```

① Handy function to serialize a map

② The converse of serializing

Wrapping the serializing/deserializing logic into utility functions can prove to be beneficial as we will see soon. Also, turns out, maps "iterability" proves once again to be our friend.

---

[4]http://json.org/

However, if this has you a tad concerned, then you are not alone. The lack of support for maps at the data-exchange layer shifts the onus of knowing what is or isn't a map to the application layer. In other words, simply looking at the JSON in no way suggests that something should be read in as a map vs. simply being an array of arrays.

Furthermore, we can no longer simply use `JSON.stringify` on an object or an array if there is a chance that it contains a map! We are now forced to interrogate all the values and if it happens to be a map, use our handy functions to first serialize that value, and only then serialize the parent. Alternatively we could try to use a third-party library[5] to do the conversion for us.[6]

The catch here is that keys for maps can be of *any* type, including references. Let us contrast this with serializing objects; keys in objects are always strings, which evaluate to themselves. Therefore, serializing an object key simply distills down to putting the string itself in JSON. Not so much with maps! If we were to use an object reference as a key in a map, and that reference were to be serialized, upon deserialization that reference is lost! Consider the following:

```
const obj = {
  name: 'some object',
};

const map = new Map([
  [obj, 'value against an object key'],
]);

const mapToJson = m => JSON.stringify([...m]);
const jsonToMap = mapStr => new Map(JSON.parse(mapStr));

const serialized = mapToJson(map); ①
// prints '[[{"name":"some object"},"value against an object key"]]'
console.log(serialized);

const deserialized = jsonToMap(serialized); ②
// prints 'Map { { name: 'some object' } => 'value against an object key'
}'
```

---

[5]https://github.com/JSON8/JSON8#ooserialize

[6]Even this does not quite do it for us. At the time of writing, this JSON can only serialize maps if their keys are strings. The reason for this I will explain next.

```
console.log(deserialized);
console.assert(deserialized.get(obj) === undefined); ③
```

① Serialize a map containing an object reference as a key

② Deserialize it back into a map

③ Lookup for the object reference fails

The only way to get back a reference to a key that itself happens to be an object reference after deserializing from JSON is to iterate over the keys of the map and grab a reference to it. Which completely defeats the purpose of a key lookup!

So, is there a real use-case for maps? Absolutely. As long as we do not intend to serialize the map, they are useful. They give the flexibility that otherwise is not permitted in plain old JavaScript objects (POJOs). Of course, if you *do* plan on serializing, then it best be that all the keys are themselves serializable (in other words, strings) so that we can "refind" them. If that is not a viable option, then you are better off just using POJOs.

# WeakMaps

ES6 introduces another variant of maps, namely `WeakMaps`. We won't spend too much time with weakmaps, except to highlight how they differ from regular maps.

The first difference is that keys in `WeakMaps` **have** to be objects; primitives are **not** allowed.[7]

The second difference lies in how weakmaps hold on to their keys. (Regular) Maps maintain a "hard" reference to their keys. For expository purposes, let us assume we had an object, and we used that object as key in a regular map. If we were maintaining a reference count of the number of references to that object, we would have to increment it by one. In other words, even if every other reference to that object were lost, the object **cannot** be garbage collected because the reference count stands at one—the one being the one the map holds on to. In order to make that key and its associated value available for garbage collection, we have to explicitly `delete` it from the map. Consider the following:

---

[7]`Symbols`, a new data type introduced in ES6 which we will cover soon are also **not** allowed.

90

```
let obj = {
  name: 'some object',
}; ①

const map = new Map([
  [obj, 'value against an object key'], ②
]);

console.assert(map.has(obj));

obj = null; ③

console.assert(map.size === 1); ④
```

① A reference to an object

② Use that reference as the key in a map

③ Drop the reference to the object

④ Map continues to hold the reference

On the other hand, weakmaps do **not** hold a hard reference to any of their keys. Instead, they hold on to their keys "weakly." One way to think about weak references is that they are too weak to force the "reference" object to stay in memory. This allows for the objects that act as their keys to be garbage collected if all *other* references to the key are lost.

Let us break this down. Let's say we have a DOM element we wish to associate some additional data with using an array. Sounds like an ideal place for a map, right? So, we use the DOM element as the key in a map, and the associated array as its value. Now anytime we want to retrieve the data we simply get the DOM element from the map and voilà, we have what we need. Perfect.

Now, some user interaction causes the element to be deleted from the DOM thus eliminating the need to hold on to the array. With the map holding a (hard) reference to that DOM element, the garbage collector cannot collect it, leaving it incumbent on us, the developers, to remember to delete the key from the map. If we *were* to forget, well there's our memory leak!

This is an ideal scenario for a weakmap. If instead we had used a weakmap to store the DOM to array key-value pair, upon deletion of the DOM element, the weakmap would allow the garbage collector to sweep away the key, and consequently the array associated with it. We are freed from having to remove the reference and its associated data from the map.

The weakmap API is rather sparse, for the simple reason that the weakmap could lose a key (and its associated value) at any point. Thus, *any* API that forces the weakmap to look at all of its entries, such as `size` and any iterative APIs, is simply impossible. Weakmaps only allow for `set`-ing, `get`-ing, and `delete`-ing keys and checking to see if the weakmap `has` an entry for a key. The weakmap constructor interface mirrors that of maps, and can take an iterable if we have one handy to hydrate the weakmap at construction time.

`WeakMaps` are primarily targeted toward library and framework authors. Think of jQuery's `data` API that lets you attach arbitrary data to any element, or if you wish to store some metadata about an object outside of the object itself (think canonical caches) and you will find a use-case for weakmaps. I am certain that we are going to see other interesting uses of weakmaps as ES6 adoption grows.

# Sets

Sets allow us to store unique items. If we attempt to add a value to a set that it already contains, then the value is simply rejected. From an implementation perspective, sets *are* maps under the covers, except that the key and value happen to be one and the same, that is, the value. This means that all of the characteristics (and caveats) of maps apply to sets as well. Maps and sets being so alike, our journey in the world of sets is going to be pretty concise.

Like maps, sets also do not offer us a literal, rather just a constructor. The set API is thorough, allowing us to work with sets just as we would expect.

We will start with construction, and working with values:

```
const obj = {};
const set = new Set(); ①

set.add('string'); ②
set.add(true);

set.add(1).add(obj); ③

console.assert(set.size === 4);

console.assert(set.has(1)); ④
```

```
set.add(1); ⑤
console.assert(set.size === 4); ⑥

console.assert(set.delete('string')); ⑦
console.assert(set.has('string') === false);

console.assert(set.delete({}) === false); ⑧
```

① Constructor to create a set

② add a value

③ add is a fluent API returning the map itself

④ has implies possession

⑤ Force a collision …

⑥ Leaving the set unchanged

⑦ If an existing value is deleted then the map returns true

⑧ Deletion of a nonexistent value returns false

There are no surprises here, and much like maps, sets offer us a complete API to work with values, providing the fluency that we have in maps as well. Of course, we must note the lack of a get which for a set is equivalent to a has (since the keys *are* the values).

Sets also offer a higher-level API that allows us to work with the set as a whole. There is a complementary constructor that accepts an iterable, with each value in the iterable representing a value in the set (assuming no collisions). The construction via an iterable should be an indicator that, like maps, sets to maintain the order of insertion (assuming no conflicts) thereby supporting iterative APIs such as 'forEach':

```
const set = new Set([ ①
  'string',
  true,
  1, ②
]);

console.assert(set.size === 3); ③

console.assert(set.has('string'));
console.assert(set.has(true));
```

```
console.assert(set.has(1));

set.forEach(k => console.log(k)); ④

console.log(set.entries());
console.log(set.keys()); ⑤
console.log(set.values()); ⑥

set.clear(); ⑦
console.assert(set.size === 0);
```

① Constructor to create a set using an iterable

② Array representing values of the set

③ Again, slightly discombobulating property to interrogate for count

④ Functional API to iterate over values

⑤ Interestingly, there is a keys API that is the same as values

⑥ All of the above return iterators

⑦ An API to clear the map and set its size to zero

Sets, like maps, act like arrays, where the "index" and the value at that index are the same. We can pass a two-argument callback to forEach on a set like so to confirm this:

```
set.forEach((k, v) => console.assert(k === v))
```

Sets also offer an entries API representing the entries in the map. Since the values in a set act as the keys, this is simply a two-length array that can be represented as [value, value]. Similarly there exist the keys and values API; however, unsurprisingly, the keys API is simply an alias for values.

Since sets are iterable, they are also spreadable. Keeping in mind that we have a constructor that takes an iterable, we have a convenient way to create new sets from existing sets, or find the union between multiple sets.

```
const colorsOne = new Set([
  'red',
  'blue',
]);
```

```
const colorsTwo = new Set([
  'yellow',
  'blue',
]);

const union = new Set([...colorsOne,  ...colorsTwo]); ①

console.assert(union.has('red'));
console.assert(union.has('blue')); ②
console.assert(union.has('yellow'));
```

① Union of two sets

② Duplicates are discarded

Finally, equality is established via the === operator, just like for maps. In other words, if we were to add a value that returned true for an === check against any existing value in the set, it simply isn't added to the set.

## Caveats

Sets *are* maps under the covers, so to go further would only belabor the point: everything that we discussed for maps applies to sets. The lack of a literal forces us to use the constructor, and since there is no support in JSON for sets, going to and from JSON might cause us to lose some fidelity.

The only difference between serializing sets vs. maps is that sets serialize to simply an array of distinct values.

## WeakSets

WeakSets are to sets as weakmaps are to maps. They provide a means for us to hold on to references "weakly," allowing their values to be garbage collected if no other references to that particular value exist.

Weaksets offer no iterative APIs as one would expect leaving only the ability to add and delete values, and check for possession via the has method. Their constructors mirror that of sets, in that they are capable of taking an iterable at construction time.

One use-case for weaksets is that of "tagging" objects. Let's say we had to serialize a JavaScript object that contained circular references. `JSON.stringify` will result in us blowing the stack. In a situation like this, we have to manually recurse through the object and its references—each time "recording" if we have seen a particular object before, and if so, not serializing that reference. A weakmap can be used to tag already seen objects, and we can be certain that there will not be any lingering references to clean up after the fact. Observe:

```
let weakSet = new WeakSet();
const replacer = (key, value) => {
  if (typeof value === 'object' && value !== null) {
    if (weakSet.has(value)) {
      // Circular reference found, discard key
      return; ①
    }
    // Store value in our collection
    weakSet.add(value);
  }
  return value;
}; ②

const rootObj = {
  name: 'rootObj',
};

rootObj.children = [{
    parent: rootObj,
    name: 'childOne',
    children: [],
  }, {
    parent: rootObj,
    name: 'childTwo',
    children: [],
}]; ③

// console.log(JSON.stringify(rootObj)); ④
console.log(JSON.stringify(rootObj, replacer, 2)); ⑤
```

```
// prints
// {
//    "name": "rootObj",
//    "children": [
//      {
//        "name": "childOne",
//        "children": []
//      },
//      {
//        "name": "childTwo",
//        "children": []
//      }
//    ]
// }
```

① If we have already encountered the key, we simply return here

② Create a replacer function for JSON.stringify

③ Create a circular reference object

④ This will fail with a stack overflow error

⑤ Use the replacer function that discards any previously seen entries

We start by writing our "replacer" function that will be invoked by JSON.stringify. As JSON.stringify recurses through the object supplied to it as the first argument to stringify, it will invoke our function, passing it the key and value that it is currently attempting to convert to a string representation. Our first check is to see if we have already "seen" that key before, by asking our internal weakset if it has that key—if it does, we simply return. Otherwise, we *first* add the key to our weakset, then proceed to return the "value." Of course, we could simply use an array to keep a list of references that we have seen previously, but then we would have to clear the array, or deference it completely, in order to ensure that we don't leak memory.

# Summary

JavaScript seems to have finally grown up. We now have at our disposal the four data-structures that we are used to in many other languages. Maps and sets fulfill a role that was previously hard to accomplish natively in JavaScript.

Both maps and sets come with some limitations. However, these limitations exist to preserve the semantics of the language (and JSON). Despite these, they prove to be a great addition to the language, allowing us, the developers, to better express our intentions in code.

In the next chapter we will look at the enhanced object literals, and explore some of the new Object APIs that were introduced in ES6.

# CHAPTER 7

# Bright Shiny Object(s) using Enhanced Object Literals

The literal object syntax ({}) in JavaScript is a powerful mechanism that allows us to describe objects *literally in code*. This {} syntax is rather elegant, and succinct; however, there remain a few warts—defining methods can be a tad verbose, and tacking on computed properties is at best clumsy. ES6 supercharges this syntax, giving us a way to initialize properties and methods even *more* concisely, while simultaneously elevating the ability to define computed properties to a first-class citizen.

In this chapter we will see how these enhancements make building objects in JavaScript far less verbose. We will also examine the new syntax that is permitted for adding computed properties on objects, making meta-programming in JavaScript a little easier to work with. Finally, we will look at the benefits of using trailing commas, and the recent addition in ES7 that expands the use of this feature for function definitions and invocations. By the end of this chapter, we will have added some more tools in our toolkit to make our code more consistent, and less verbose.

© Raju Gandhi 2019
R. Gandhi, *JavaScript Next*, https://doi.org/10.1007/978-1-4842-5394-6_7

# The Limitations of the Object Literal

The use of the object literal syntax {} in idiomatic JavaScript code is pervasive. However, there are, in particular, three shortcomings that we will be discussing:

1. The lack of symmetry between getters/setters and object methods

2. The inability to list a computed property within the literal syntax

3. The verbosity that often accompanies defining object properties using variables

Let us examine each of these separately.

## Getter/setters vs. Methods

Objects in JavaScript are permitted to have get-ters and set-ters defined alongside methods. The difference between the two happens to be the invocation pattern—getters and setters while being functions are not invoked as such. Rather, their behavior is in line with how we work with properties. Consider the following example that attempts to highlight the differences in the usage patterns between the two:

```
const song = {
  name: 'Yellow Submarine', ①
  get duration() { ②
    console.log('Getter is invoked');
    return this._duration ? (this._duration / 60) : 0;
  },
  set duration(inMin) { ③
    if (inMin <= 0) { ④
      throw new Error('duration of song cannot be less or equal to 0 min');
    }
    console.log(`Setter is invoked with ${inMin}`);
    this._duration = inMin * 60; ⑤
  },
  getName: function () { ⑥
    return this.name;
  },
};
```

```
console.assert(song.name === 'Yellow Submarine'); ⑦

// song.duration = -1; ⑧
song.duration = 3.00; ⑨
console.assert(song.duration === 3); ⑩

console.assert(song.getName() === 'Yellow Submarine'); ⑪
```

① Introduce a property

② Create a get method

③ A set-ter method

④ Validate the input

⑤ Store it differently

⑥ A traditional method

⑦ Property lookup

⑧ This will produce a validation error

⑨ Invokes the set method

⑩ Invokes the get method

⑪ Invoke a regular method

As one might surmise, getters and setters, often referred to as "virtual attributes," allow us to implement hooks in what otherwise seem to be property lookups. These hooks can be used for a variety of use-cases, including validation and sanitization of inputs, or modifying attributes on the way out as previously demonstrated. This difference is apparent when we compare reading (get-ting) and set-ting duration to invoking the object method getName.

The key issue here is that although they are all defined as methods on an object, there is a lack of symmetry between how we define getters and setters and defining methods. While the former involves a rather elegant and perhaps even familiar syntax to programmers coming in from other languages, the latter continues to make use of the traditional key-value syntax.

# Defining Computed Properties on Object Literals

Objects in JavaScript also permit keys to be "computed" at runtime, allowing for some level of meta-programming facilities in JavaScript. In order to tack on a computed property on an object we are to use the "bracket" (or subscript) notation on an existing object, like so:

```
const getterFor = (prop) => { ①
  const capitalized = prop.charAt(0).toUpperCase() + prop.slice(1); ②
  return `get${capitalized}`;
};

const song = {
  name: 'All You Need Is Love',
  album: 'Yellow Submarine',
};

song[getterFor('name')] = function() { ③
  return song['name'];
};

song[getterFor('album')] = function() {
  return song['album'];
};

console.assert(song.getName() === song.name);
console.assert(song.getAlbum() === song.album);
```

① A function to create a name from a property

② Capitalize the name of the supplied property

③ Use the subscript syntax to tack on the calculated method name an object

In this example we start with a simple helper function that calculates the name of the getter given a property name. Given the property, say name, getterFor('name') simply returns getName.

As we can see, bracket notation provides us a way to evaluate any *expression* to calculate the name of the soon-to-be object key, and attach it to the object. However, we have to do this outside of the {} object notation, since the syntax does not afford us a means to do that inline, like we do other properties. This forces us to have the "complete" object definition scattered in several different places.

## Defining Object Properties Using Variables

Idiomatic JavaScript leverages object literals *everywhere*, from encapsulating private members and exposing public APIs using the "revealing module pattern" to Node exports. There is often a large amount of duplication that results from using object literals in this manner. Observe:

```
const greeter = (function () {
  let greeting = 'Hello'; ①

  const exclaim = msg => `${msg}!`; ②

  const greet = name => exclaim(`${greeting} ${name}`);

  const salutation = (newGreeting) => {
    greeting = newGreeting;
  };

  return {
    greet: greet,
    salutation: salutation,
  }; ③
}()); ④

console.assert(greeter.greet('Mason') === 'Hello Mason!');
greeter.salutation('Hola');
console.assert(greeter.greet('Micah') === 'Hola Micah!');
```

① A private member variable

② A private function

③ Expose a specific public API on the object literal

④ Wrap the object creation in an IEFE to encapsulate private members within function scope

103

The revealing module pattern leverages the fact that functions introduce scope. We start with an "Immediately Executing Function Expression" (IEFE). Within the IEFE we are free to define any number of "private" members and functions, which are scoped to the enclosing function. At the end of the IEFE, we simply create a new object via the literal syntax, and have its properties point to the members that are to be part of the public API. As we observe there is a fair amount of duplication, for example, `greet: greet` that stems out of this implementation. If this were a far more elaborate implementation, it proves to be not only verbose, but error-prone as well.

Now that we have seen some use-cases for the literal object, let us explore how ES6 attempts to overcome these using the "enhanced" object literal syntax.

# Enhanced Object Literal Syntax

The enhancements to the object literal syntax in ES6 simply aims to simplify how we define properties and methods within our literal object definitions.

## Method Definition Shorthand

The object literal syntax introduces a shorthand for method definitions within the literal syntax, bringing it to parity with getter/setter definitions. We revisit our earlier example, except this time using the shortcut:

```
const song = {
  name: 'Yellow Submarine', ①
  get duration() { ②
    console.log('Getter is invoked');
    return this._duration ? (this._duration / 60) : 0;
  },
  set duration(inMin) { ③
    if (inMin <= 0) { ④
    throw new Error('duration of song cannot be less or equal to 0 min');
  }
  console.log(`Setter is invoked with ${inMin}`);
  this._duration = inMin * 60; ⑤
},
```

```
  getName() { ①
    return this.name;
  },
  setName(name) { ②
    this.name = name;
  },
};

console.assert(song.getName() === 'Yellow Submarine');
song.setName('All You Need Is Love');
console.assert(song.getName() === 'All You Need Is Love');
```

① Use the method shorthand to define a regular function

② Define a method that takes an argument

This example is no different than our earlier stab at the same—however, the definition of getName (and setName) is significantly less verbose. Gone is the : and the function keyword; all that remains is the method implementation. We now find symmetry between any method definition on a literal, be that getters/setters or regular methods.

## Computed Values

The computed values enhancement lets us *move* the definition of computed properties within the literal syntax, avoiding scattering the definition of literals in different places within the codebase. We come back to our earlier example except to use inline computed values this time around:

```
const getterFor = (prop) => { ①
  const capitalized = prop.charAt(0).toUpperCase() + prop.slice(1); ②
  return `get${capitalized}`;
};

const song = {
  name: 'All You Need Is Love',
  album: 'Yellow Submarine',
  [getterFor('name')]() { ③
```

```
    return song.name;
  },
  [getterFor('album')]() {
    return song.album;
  },
};

console.assert(song.getName() === song.name);
console.assert(song.getAlbum() === song.album);
```

① A function to create a name from a property

② Split the name to get the first character

③ Inline the computed definition

This enhancement lets us define a computed property just as we would have, that is, using the bracket notation, except that the brackets find themselves inside the literal, making them first class like any other property definition. The new syntax also adapts the symmetry introduced by the method definition shorthand, allowing us to avoid the superfluous `function` keyword. Likewise, if we were defining a property vs. a method, the familiar `key:value` syntax applies here just as it does for traditional keys except the computation of the key name would still be enclosed within square brackets. Therefore, the equivalent for computed properties would be `[computedKey]:value`.

## Property Value Shorthand

The value shorthand, rather than being a new way to define properties (and methods), provides a way to reduce the verbosity often seen in the revealing module pattern, or Node `exports`. It lets us condense the definition of a key-value pair in an object literal only if the name of the key matches an existing variable in scope.

We revisit our revealing module pattern definition, but this time using the value shorthand:

```
const greeter = (function() {
  let  greeting = 'Hello';

  const exclaim = msg => `${msg}!`;

  const greet = name => exclaim(`${greeting} ${name}`);
```

```
  const salutation = (newGreeting) => {
    greeting = newGreeting;
  };

  return {
    greet, ①
    salutation,
  };
  // equivalent to
  /*
  return {
    greet: greet,
    salutation: salutation
  }
  */
}());

console.assert(greeter.greet('Mason') === 'Hello Mason!');
greeter.salutation('Hola');
console.assert(greeter.greet('Micah') === 'Hola Micah!');
```

① Use the property value shorthand

In this example, the properties (keys) introduced in the (returned) module have the same name as their values—we are now allowed to eliminate the duplication using the shorthand syntax. Of course, we are allowed to mix and match the property value shorthand alongside the familiar key:value notation we are used to if need be. This is handy if the names of certain keys in the object being returned do **not** line up with the name of any variables in scope.

This may seem like a small win, but if we were to extrapolate the gains for large modules, perhaps we can see how much repetition we can avoid, thus embracing DRY and avoiding potential bugs introduced by typos.

# The Case of the Trailing Comma

JavaScript has permitted "trailing commas" in array and object literals for a while now:

```
const friedmanBooks = [
  'The Little Schemer',
  'The Seasoned Schemer',
  'The Reasoned Schemer', ①
];

const hoyteBook = {
  name: 'Let Over Lambda',
  author: 'Doug Hoyte',
  isbn10: '1435712757', ②
};
```

① The trailing comma in array literals

② The trailing comma in object literals

Trailing commas as a feature might seem trite, but they pack a powerful punch. They make our code consistent, in that every line in an array or object definition looks the same. This makes it easy to reorder items in literals, and produces cleaner diffs in version control systems if items are added or removed, particularly at the end of literals.

ES7 brought trailing commas to function parameter lists, and function invocations:

```
const rate = (
  book,
  starCount, ①
) => `You rated '${book}' ${starCount} stars`;

const rating = rate(
  'Practical Common Lisp',
  5, ②
);
// prints 'You rated 'Practical Common Lisp' 5 stars'
console.log(rating);
```

① The trailing comma in function parameter list

② The trailing comma in function invocations

This addition aims to bring parity, and consequently all the benefits of trailing commas to function definitions and invocations.

Ostensibly trailing commas only add value if the elements are listed on new-lines. As a result, it is preferred to enforce trailing commas only if the element (or object property) is on a line of its own. Most linters like ESLint[1] can be configured to flag missing trailing commas only on multiline declarations.

# Summary

ES6 introduces a slew of new syntax and APIs that make creating new objects, both literally, and from existing objects easier, less verbose, and less error-prone.

In the next chapter we will explore Symbols, a new primitive type introduced in ES6, that are typically used in conjunction with the enhanced literal syntax, both as a mechanism to introduce "unique" keys in an object and modifying the behavior of your objects via metaprogramming.

---

[1]`https://eslint.org/docs/rules/comma-dangle`

# CHAPTER 8

# Hiding Behind Symbols

## Introduction

Property naming in JavaScript objects presents one major obstacle, especially when working with third-party libraries or frameworks, which is, property name collisions. We have surrendered to the idea that we will be constrained in how we can or cannot name our variables and properties. Warning such as "Do not use $ prefix for the names of variables, properties and methods. This prefix is reserved for <INSERT FRAMEWORK/LIBRARY NAME HERE> usage" are common, and something we just take in stride.

Well no more!

In this chapter, we will see how a new data type introduced in ES6, namely `Symbol`, helps us eliminate this obstacle, freeing us from this constraint, and allowing us to lay out our objects as we wish, knowing that we will not in any way be limited with what or how we can use them in whatever setting that we wish to. We will also see how we can modify the behavior of built-in operations like `String.match` and `String.split` using `Symbols`. By the end of this chapter we will have freed ourselves from the tyranny of enforced naming conventions, leaving us dancing alongside all libraries and frameworks, not to mention JavaScript itself, as one happy family.

## The Inability to Enforce a Contract

Let's say we are making use of a third-party library in our code, and it exposes a function that expects the objects you supply it to have a property with a *specific* name. Consider a simple example:

```
const LOG_LEVEL = 'log'; ①
const DEBUG = 'DEBUG';
const INFO = 'INFO';
const ERROR = 'ERROR';
```

© Raju Gandhi 2019
R. Gandhi, *JavaScript Next*, https://doi.org/10.1007/978-1-4842-5394-6_8

```
const simpleLogger = (obj, msg) => {
  let returnMsg;
  switch (obj[LOG_LEVEL]) { ②
    case DEBUG:
      returnMsg = `DEBUG: ${msg}`;
      break;
    case INFO:
      returnMsg = `INFO: ${msg}`;
      break;
    case ERROR:
      returnMsg = `ERROR: ${msg}`;
      break;
    default:
      throw new Error('Invalid LOG_LEVEL');
  }
  console.log(returnMsg);
  return returnMsg;
};

const loggableObj = {
  [LOG_LEVEL]: INFO, ③
};

simpleLogger(loggableObj, 'this is a test');

const someOtherObject = {
  log: 'this is just an ordinary property', ④
};

// simpleLogger(someOtherObject, 'some message') ⑤
```

① Convenient const to make things easier

② Look up the property the implementation expects to find on the supplied object

③ Tack a property on a simple object so it can be used by simpleLogger

④ Another object that just happens to have a `log` property

⑤ Now what do we do?

In this example, the library function expects that any object supplied to it must have a property called `log`. The library conveniently gives us a `const` we can use along with the enhanced literal syntax to tack the appropriate property on our objects. Internally, the `simpleLogger` function interrogates the `log` property to establish the logging level, and then prints out the appropriate message.

But what if our object already has a name property called `log` that serves a completely different purpose? That is, our intention with the `log` property collides with how the function expects it to be used. So, we can either choose to replace ours to accommodate the needs of the library or choose not to use the library altogether. None of those seem like great options.

The issue here is although we have `const`, which allows us to safely reference a "name" that we will always get the right *value*, strings and consequently object keys (be that property or method) *can* collide! This is the reason why often libraries that introduce and/or expect "special" properties on other objects use a naming convention—like prefixing the injected properties with a _ or a $, and decreeing that developers that use that library should **not** use the same prefix within their code. Consider the AngularJS style guide,[1] which explicitly states the following:

> Do not use $ prefix for the names of variables, properties and methods. This prefix is reserved for AngularJS usage.

The dilemma presented here is that in order to address our needs, we need a way to define a *name* that has no chance of a collision, in other words, a truly unique name that does not, and cannot, in any way impugn with any existing names or properties. Furthermore, we wish to do this without being forced to enforce coding policies, or even worse, use some arcane naming policy like the use UUIDs to avoid conflicts!

---

[1]https://github.com/mgechev/angularjs-style-guide

# Symbols to the Rescue

Symbols are a **new** primitive type that was introduced in ES6. Much like other primitives, symbols have a wrapper type, named Symbol, which offers a factory function to initialize new symbols. Unlike other wrapper objects like String, we are **not** allowed to new a symbol—that is, using new Symbol() will result in an error. Let us look at a snippet of code to see how we can go about initializing symbols:

```
const symbol1 = Symbol();
const symbol2 = Symbol(); ①
console.assert(symbol1 !== symbol2); ②

const symbol3 = Symbol('unique'); ③
// prints Symbol(unique)
console.log(symbol3); ④
```

① Use the factory function to create a new symbol

② Two symbols never equal each other

③ For debugging purposes, a description can be supplied to a symbol

④ Symbols have a toString implementation that displays the description if provided

The Symbol initializer can be provided with a description; however, this description has no effect on the symbol being created, other than it being useful for debugging purposes.

Two symbols can **never** be equal to one another—every invocation of the Symbol initializer returns a new and unique Symbol instance. This is true *even if* the description provided is the same (because like we have discussed, the string provided to the initializing function is merely for debugging).

So, we now have a way to create a unique "thing." How does that help us with naming collisions?

Well, it turns out, we can use symbols as keys in objects! Let us start with seeing how we can use both symbols and strings to define properties on objects:

```
const ITERATOR = Symbol('iterator'); ①

const iterableObject = {
  name: 'iterable',
}; ②

iterableObject[ITERATOR] = function() {
  return 'I am iterable';
}; ③

const objWithExistingKey = {
  iterator: 'some value',
}; ④

objWithExistingKey[ITERATOR] = () => 'Works!'; ⑤
```

① Define a symbol

② A plain JavaScript object with only a name property

③ Tack on the `iterable` property with no collisions

④ This object already has a property with the `iterator` name

⑤ We can still tack on a symbol with the description `iterator` with no collision

Note that we first create a symbol—we then use that *reference* as the name of a property on the object, as well as for lookup. As demonstrated, we can use the subscript syntax to tack on a new property on an existing object just like we would have done with any expression. Lastly, an object can have a combination of strings and symbols as its properties, even if the name of the property matches the description of the symbol.

Using our new found knowledge, let us revisit our `simpleLogger` to see how we use symbols to "sprinkle" behavior on objects where previously we would have to simply submit to the consequences of name collisions.

```
const LOG_LEVEL = Symbol('log'); ①
const DEBUG = 'DEBUG';
const INFO = 'INFO';
const ERROR = 'ERROR';
```

```
const simpleLogger = (obj, msg) => {
  let returnMsg;
  switch (obj[LOG_LEVEL]) { ②
    case DEBUG:
      returnMsg = `DEBUG: ${msg}`;
      break;
    case INFO:
      returnMsg = `INFO: ${msg}`;
      break;
    case ERROR:
      returnMsg = `ERROR: ${msg}`;
      break;
    default:
      throw new Error('Invalid LOG_LEVEL');
  }
  console.log(returnMsg);
  return returnMsg;
};

const loggableObj = {
  log: 'this is just an ordinary property',
  [LOG_LEVEL]: INFO, ③
};

simpleLogger(loggableObj, 'this is a test'); ④
```

① Define LOG_LEVEL as a symbol

② Look up the required property in the switch

③ Introduce a property using the symbol reference

④ Now it works!

This example highlights how we can use symbols to introduce conflict-free properties on new or existing objects.

Using symbols to define "interface" or "contract" properties frees library and function writers from having to mandate coding conventions, while simultaneously allowing clients using these libraries to design their objects as they deem fit, and yet be able to use these libraries without fear of collisions.

Win–win!

## Symbols and Switch-cases

We can consider another use-case where having unique values (symbols) can help mitigate potential bugs. We often use strings to identify "uniqueness," and language constructs like switch-case utilize this to aid in program flow. Consider the following:

```
const LOG_LEVEL = Symbol('log');
const DEBUG = 'DEBUG'; ①
const INFO = 'INFO';
const ERROR = 'ERROR';

const simpleLogger = (obj, msg) => {
  let returnMsg;
  switch (obj[LOG_LEVEL]) { ②
    case DEBUG:
      returnMsg = `DEBUG: ${msg}`;
      break;
    case INFO:
      returnMsg = `INFO: ${msg}`;
      break;
    case ERROR:
      returnMsg = `ERROR: ${msg}`;
      break;
    default:
      throw new Error('Invalid LOG_LEVEL');
}
  console.log(returnMsg);
  return returnMsg;
};

const MY_LEVEL = 'ERROR'; ③
const loggableObj = {
```

```
  log: 'this is just an ordinary property',
  [LOG_LEVEL]: MY_LEVEL, ④
};

// prints 'ERROR: this is a test'
  simpleLogger(loggableObj, 'this is a test'); ⑤
```

① Define helper constants

② Switch case over a string property

③ Introduce a misleading constant

④ Use the misleading constant as a log level in a new object

⑤ The output is not as expected

It takes an astute reader to realize what happened here. We introduce a misleading constant, namely MY_LEVEL which evaluates to "ERROR", and assign it as the LOG_LEVEL to an object. This works, because within the simpleLogger function, the switch-case evaluates for *equality*, matching on the ERROR case because the supplied LOG_LEVEL just so happens to have a value that we know of. However, instead of throwing an error, we successfully log an error message. The issue here is that while strings *are* values, two separately constructed strings can be equal if they happen to have the same set of characters with the same casing!

Ideally, we would like to be able to create truly unique values that we can use to switch between. Well, it turns out that the switch statement in JavaScript simply uses the === equality operator to find a matching case! Again, symbols to the rescue.

```
const LOG_LEVEL = Symbol('log');
const DEBUG = Symbol('DEBUG'); ①
const INFO = Symbol('INFO');
const ERROR = Symbol('ERROR');

const simpleLogger = (obj, msg) => {
  let returnMsg;
  switch (obj[LOG_LEVEL]) { ②
  case DEBUG:
    returnMsg = `DEBUG: ${msg}`;
    break;
  case INFO:
```

```
    returnMsg = `INFO: ${msg}`;
    break;
  case ERROR:
    returnMsg = `ERROR: ${msg}`;
    break;
  default:
    throw new Error('Invalid LOG_LEVEL');
}
  console.log(returnMsg);
  return returnMsg;
};

const loggableObj = {
  log: 'this is just an ordinary property',
  [LOG_LEVEL]: ERROR,
};

// prints 'ERROR: this is a test'
simpleLogger(loggableObj, 'this is a test'); ③
```

① Define helper constants as symbols instead of strings

② Notice the switch case does **not** change

③ This works just like it did with strings

Recall that symbols are unique, and that every call to the initializer function Symbol creates a new and unique symbol object, which does not equal any other symbol (even those with the same description string). In our latest iteration, we use symbols as the key to uniquely identify the LOG_LEVEL, as well as its value, which we can now guarantee to be unique.

# Global Registry

There is yet another facet of Symbols that we should talk about, namely the global symbol registry. We can think of the symbol registry as a pool of symbols—you can create and put a symbol in the pool, and retrieve it later.

To create and or fetch a symbol from the pool, we use `Symbol.for`. `Symbol.for` expects to be supplied a "key," and if a symbol with that key does **not** exist in the registry, then one will be created. Otherwise, a symbol with the same key is retrieved from the registry, like so:

```
const global = Symbol.for('globally visible'); ①
const otherGlobal = Symbol.for('globally visible'); ②

// prints 'true'
console.log(global === otherGlobal); ③
```

① Define a symbol using `for`—In this case a symbol will be created

② Look up a symbol using the same "key"—This is simply a "get" operation

③ They are equal

It turns out that for symbols in the global registry, it *is* the key that identifies the symbol—two references will point to the same symbol if they both use the same key to look up a symbol using `for`.

We can also go the other way—given a symbol, we can fetch its key using `keyFor` method on Symbol.

```
const global = Symbol.for('a unique key'); ①
const key = Symbol.keyFor(global); ②

// prints 'true'
console.log(key === 'a unique key');
```

① Define a symbol using `for`—In this case a symbol will be created

② Look up the key for a particular symbol

You might be wondering—what's the point? The pool is necessary if we wanted to share symbols (which are references unlike strings, numbers, and booleans which are primitives) across "realms."[2] A realm is a global context, such as one that exists in an iframe. So, the JavaScript code running in a webpage runs in a different realm that

---

[2]For other primitives an equality check is a value check. Therefore, the string "es6" in one realm equals the string "es6" in another realm thus avoiding the need to have a registry for them.

the code that runs in an embedded iframe, or code that runs in a service worker. If we wanted to use symbols as global identifiers, or names of properties that crossed realms, then the global symbol registry is your friend.

Of course, to identify a symbol in the global registry, we need a key. There is always a chance that two disparate pieces of code (even those running in different realms) might use the same key (for different purposes) to create a symbol. Thus it behooves us to appropriately "namespace" any such identifiers if we are to use the global registry.

# Well-known Symbols

JavaScript ships with a set of useful symbols, tacked on as "static" properties on the Symbol type. The primary objective of these "well-known symbols" is to allow us, the developers, to customize how certain algorithms work with our objects.

Let us take a step back and reconsider what we learned. One, symbols allow us to introduce collision-free properties on our objects, and two, library function authors can now freely assemble a list of symbols that they define, and *ask* that we use these symbols within our objects if we wish to use that library.

Well, with well-known symbols, JavaScript, the language *is* the library!

Let's crystallize this with a concrete example. JavaScript strings have a method called "split," which given a separator (and an optional limit) will tokenize the string at the separator, returning an array of individual strings.

```
const url = 'https://admin:supersecret@gitlab.com/looselytyped/sample-repo.
git'; ①
const split = url.match(/\w+:\w+/); ②
// prints
// [
//    'admin:supersecret',
//    index: 8,
//    input: 'https://admin:supersecret@gitlab.com/looselytyped/sample-repo.
     git',
//    groups: undefined
// ]
console.log(split);
```

① Define a URL with a username and password encoded

② Use a regular expression to extract the username and password combination

We use a simple regular expression to extract the username and password encoded in a URL string. Except, the password is being displayed in plain text! What if we wanted to change or augment each match prior to placing them in the array?

The obvious solution is we obfuscate the password *after* matching it using our regular expression. However, this separates the act of extracting the username and password, and the obfuscation of the password itself.

Perhaps we could obfuscate the password *during* the "match." It turns out that String.match method can be supplied an object as an argument (instead of a regular expression), and if the supplied object implements a method with the name that evaluates to Symbol.match, then String.match will simply forward the call to that method. Observe:

```
const passwordObfuscator = {  ①
  regex: /\w+:\w+/,
  [Symbol.match](str) {  ②
    const creds = str.match(this.regex);
    if (creds) {
      const [username] = creds[0].split(':');  ③
      return [
        `${username}:**********`,  ④
      ];
    }
    return creds;
  },
};
```

```
const url = 'https://admin:supersecret@gitlab.com/looselytyped/sample-repo.git';
const credentials = url.match(passwordObfuscator);  ⑤
```

```
// prints 'obfuscated credentials [ 'admin:***********' ]'
console.log('obfuscated credentials', credentials);
```

    ① Define a custom object

    ② Define a method on the object using the `Symbol.match`

    ③ Extract the username from the match

    ④ Return a new array that holds the username while obfuscate the password

    ⑤ Supply the custom matcher to the `match` method

We define an object, and use the enhanced object literal syntax to tack on a method with the name that evaluates to `Symbol.match`.[3] By implementing `Symbol.match`, our object is abiding by the contract that `String.match` expects. `match` can now delegate the act of matching to our object—rather than doing the match itself, it simply invokes `passwordObfuscator[Symbol.match]`. Internal to our implementation, we first extract the username from the string (coincidentally using `match` again except this time we supply it with a regular expression[4]), obfuscate the password, and return it.

Granted this example is nowhere near production grade, it does serve to highlight how we can use these well-known symbols to modify the behavior of existing APIs in JavaScript.

The `Symbol` object has many more static members that serve to change how JavaScript works with our objects. There is `Symbol.iterator` which we will see soon in our discussion of generators and iterators. There is also `Symbol.primitive` that allows us to define how an object should be coerced by JavaScript to a primitive. You can find a list of all these on MDN web docs under the Symbol reference page.[5]

---

[3]Note that we do not care what `Symbol.match` evaluates to. We simply wish that the method we introduce has a name that `String.match` expects it to have.

[4]Regular expression objects also implement `Symbol.match`.

[5]https://developer.mozilla.org/en-US/docs/Web/JavaScript/Reference/Global_Objects/ Symbol

# Not so Private

If we were to take any object, and loop over its members using `Object.keys` (which lists all of the objects enumerable keys), or `Object.getOwnPropertyNames` (which lists all including nonenumerable keys), we will see that any members defined using symbols are not listed. Let us test this out with a simple demonstration:

```
const obj = {
  a: 'a simple property', ①
  [Symbol()]: 'a symbol property', ②
};

Object.defineProperty(obj, 'nonenumerable', { ③
  value: 'an unenumerable property',
  enumerable: false,
});

// lists only 'a'
console.log(Object.keys(obj));
// lists 'a' and 'nonenumerable'
console.log(Object.getOwnPropertyNames(obj));
// also lists only 'a'
console.log(JSON.stringify(obj)); ④
```

> ① Define an object with a string key
>
> ② Define another using a symbol
>
> ③ Define a third and unenumerable key
>
> ④ Inspect for keys

We define an object with several keys—a traditional key-value pair, another that happens to be a symbol, and finally a third using `Object.defineProperty` with the enumerable flag set to false. Running this example illustrates that we cannot see the symbol property on the object.

While this may *seem* to suggest that symbol keys are private, and to the extent that we use traditional introspection mechanisms (like `JSON.stringify`), they are indeed "private."

However, that does not mean they are, and allowing objects to have private keys is not the intent of symbol properties. ES6 introduces yet another API, namely `Object.getOwnPropertySymbols` that lists any and all symbol properties that exist on an object. Go ahead, try it on our example and you will see that it does list the one symbol property.

In summary, using a combination of methods on `Object,` we can tease out *all* the properties that exist on any object.

# Summary

In this chapter we took a deep dive into a new primitive type, namely Symbols. We investigated some limitations to using traditional keys, namely that we chance a collision and how symbols can be used to define truly unique identifiers. We also saw that the global symbol registry allows us to define and interrogate for symbols, even across JavaScript realms. We took a glance at how we can modify how JavaScript (or for that matter any API) interacts with our objects using symbols as a means to implement a "contract" between caller and callee. Finally, we closed off with how symbols, while seemingly private, aren't really private.

In the next chapter we will see a mechanism for iterating over collections, as well as how we produce and consume lazy computations and sequences.

# CHAPTER 9

# Iterable Sequences with Generators and Iterators

Storing and manipulating data in collections in JavaScript is not only easy, but also elegant. However, iterating is another matter. Consider arrays. In order to iterate and fetch the elements of an array, we use contrived syntax like the for (let i = 0; i < array.length; i++) loop, or even worse, the for-in loop. But that's not the end of it! Every so often we will have custom objects that might need iteration. We concede defeat, and build (or consume) a custom API (think array.forEach) just so we can get each element in a particular sequence.

Well those days are over.

ES6 introduces a new iteration mechanism, namely the for-of loop that makes iteration over collections easy, and consistent. ES6 also introduces the idea of iterators, that allow for any object to be iterated over using the for-of loop. Finally, we get a new kind of function, namely generators that allow us to produce iterable objects with some sweet syntactic sugar.

In this chapter we will examine the elegance, and the benefits of the for-of loop, and explore its symbiotic relationship with iterators. We will see how we can make our own objects iterable, thereby permitting their usage alongside the for-of loop.

By the end of this chapter, we will have understood the need and use for Symbol. iterator and see how it plays a role in making collections and objects iterable. We will also see how generators can be used to create iterables, both of finite and infinite length as well as allow us to write lazily evaluated code.

© Raju Gandhi 2019
R. Gandhi, *JavaScript Next*, https://doi.org/10.1007/978-1-4842-5394-6_9

# The Drawbacks of Lacking an Iteration Protocol

JavaScript, up until ES5 shipped with two data-structures: the object and the array. The object acts primarily as a key-value store, and the array as an indexed collection. ES6 introduced us to two more, namely maps and sets. JavaScript gives us some mechanisms to consume elements of these data-structures via looping or iteration; however, it lacks many of the facilities offered by other modern languages, in particular a standard API for consumption.

Take, for example, arrays. Arrays give us several ways to iterate—the imperative `for(const i = 0; i < array.length)` version, the `forEach` method that is available on the array prototype, and finally the `for-in` loop. Let us briefly consider each one.

The traditional `for` loop, while being ubiquitous, and probably the most familiar to most JavaScript programmers, is both verbose and error-prone. As Venkat Subramaniam often says (and I agree), "I can never remember if it is < or <=!". (Thank the stars for auto-completion in our IDEs, right?) However, it *does* allow us to control how much of the array we wish to iterate over, or even `break` out of the loop if we so desire to.

On the other hand, the `forEach` method that arrays offer us isn't a syntactical construct offered to us by the language, rather it is a method on the `Array` object, thereby dismissing its usage for any other indexed collection type. The `forEach` loop is designed to iterate over the entire length of the array, with no means to "break" out of the looping (unless of course we throw an `Error` which is certainly not a good solution).

Finally, there is the `for-in` loop, whose role is to iterate over the enumerable properties of an object. Using the `for-in` loop with arrays has a rather surprising outcome:

```
const arr = ['a']; ①

for (const k in arr) {
  console.assert(k === '0'); ②
  console.log(arr[k]); ③
}
```

① Define a one-item array

② Look at the type of the key

③ Use the key to get to the actual indexed value

The "key" that we get back is not a number (as one might expect for the index) but rather a string. Furthermore, since the loop only hands us keys, we are then forced to use the subscript or square-bracket notation to get to the element at that position in the array.

Of course, none of this solves the real problem at hand, which is that JavaScript inherently lacks the ability for any collection to conform to a contract that allows it to be iterated upon. We have lots of places where we get a collection of items—consider `document.querySelectorAll`, which returns a `NodeList`, or `Immutable.js`[1] which has an `Immutable.List` object. We currently have no canonical API that we reach for to look at all the items in these collections.

Considering we are speaking of iterating, another glaring omission from JavaScript is the inability to write lazily evaluated code, and consequently produce infinite sequences.

Let's pretend we are writing a math library, and we wish to write a function that produces the Fibonacci sequence. Given what we have in ES5, and what we have learned from our excursions into ES6 so far, our first attempt might look something like this:

*Naive implementation of a Fibonacci sequence generator*

```
const fibonacci = (n) => { ①
  const result = [];
  let start = 0;
  let next = 1;

  switch (n) {
    case 0:
      break;
    case 1:
      result.push(start);
      break;
    case 2:
      result.push(start);
      result.push(next);
      break;
    default:
      result.push(start);
      result.push(next);
```

---

[1]Immutable.js is a library from Facebook that offers a set of immutable collections for JavaScript.

```
    for (let i = 2; i < n; i++) {
      const val = start + next;
      start = next;
      next = val;
      result.push(val);
    }
  }
  return result;
};

// prints []
console.log(fibonacci(0));
// prints [ 0 ]
console.log(fibonacci(1));
// prints [ 0, 1 ]
console.log(fibonacci(2));
// prints [ 0, 1, 1, 2, 3, 5, 8, 13, 21, 34 ]
console.log(fibonacci(10));
```

① Define a function that expects one argument, namely n

We write a simple function that expects one argument, n that tells us how many of the sequence to generate, and then use a rather simple algorithm to produce the necessary Fibonacci sequence, each time pushing items into the resultant array. I will grant you that this is a rather naive implementation, but it suffices to serve our discussion, which centers around a rather subtle aspect, the argument to the function.

A language like Haskell is inherently lazy—in other words, code in Haskell is never evaluated unless it absolutely has to be. Languages like Clojure, and now Java (with the Stream API), provide us with data-structures that are lazy—in effect allowing us to work with lazily computed collections, and consequently, infinite collections.

Coming back to the discussion at hand, the issue here is that any client code using our library has to know *upfront* how many of the Fibonacci sequence numbers they want.[2] This shifts the onus from the library (or function) writers to the users! It provides

---

[2]I realize we could get clever and write some sort of a state machine implementation, allowing the client to move the machine to its next state if and when they choose to; however, this does not present itself as a viable solution, simply because now the client has to use the custom API for our state machine, vs. simply using say Arrays API.

no elegant mechanism for clients to determine if they want more at runtime, or simply stop consuming while they are iterating over the sequence.

However, if we *could* lazily evaluate the "next" item in the Fibonacci sequence when and *only* when the client asks us to, then we would have no reason to mandate an argument to our Fibonacci sequence generator. Instead, we would simply hand them back a data-structure, perhaps even an array, and wait patiently for them to ask for the next item in the sequence, calculate it, and return it!

Lazy evaluation and sequences offer a ton of benefits, from making code (potentially) more efficient (we will never calculate any more than we need to), simplifying APIs (no reason to ask for "how many" upfront), all while providing a very elegant solution to a range of algorithmic problems.

# The for-of Loop

ES6 introduces a brand-new looping mechanism, namely the `for-of` loop, the immediate benefit of which can be easily demonstrated:

```
const arr = ['a', 'b', 'c']; ①

for (const k of arr) { ②
  // prints 'a', 'b', 'c' in sequence
  console.log(k); ③
}
```

① Define an array

② Use the `for-of` loop

③ Print each of the items in the array

Let us pause and admire the elegance of the `for-of` loop. Gone is the imperatively indexed `for` loop. No need for the `for-in` loop either. All that remains is true intent of the code—iterate over an array to get each *element* of the array in sequence!

This works because the for-of loop can iterate over anything that happens to be "iterable," and arrays happen to be iterable in ES6. That is, they present a canonical API for iteration that allows the for-of loop to get every element in the array in the correct sequence.

And it does not end there—maps, sets, and strings all happen to be iterable, so we can use the for-of loop with all of them:

```
const array = [10, 20, 30, 40, 50];
for (const i of array) {
  console.log(i);
}

const set = new Set(['a', 'set', true, false]);
for (const i of set) {
  console.log(i);
}

const map = new Map([
  ['s', 'is a string'],
  [true, 'is a boolean'],
]);
for (const [k, v] of map) { ①
  console.log(`${k}->${v}`);
}

const string = 'ES6 is awesome!';
for (const i of string) {
  console.log(i);
}
```

> ① Considering we get a key-value pair back per iteration, we can use array destructuring

Turns out, any object or collection can participate in the for-of loop, as long as it conforms to the iterable protocol. Let us see what it means to be iterable in JavaScript.

# Iterables and Iterators

Statically typed languages like Java provide us with an interface called `Iterator`. An interface is a contract, that mandates that an object expose a specific API, and one that is enforced by the runtime. In Java, any object that "implements" the `Iterator` interface essentially declares to the world that it can be iterated upon. Similarly, dynamically typed languages like Ruby have the *idea* of a contract, essentially via convention.

Regardless of the type of language, whether static or dynamic, they offer a way to mark an object as being iterable, allowing consumers to access individual elements of that object in a standard way, and without having the need for the object to expose any of its internal implementation details. Furthermore, since accessing the elements is using a contract of some sort, the language itself can provide additional constructs (like Java's enhanced `for` loop) that utilizes the same mechanism for looping.

Typically, to be iterable, the object (or collection) **must** implement an API declaring itself to be such (e.g., in Java the object must implement the `Iterator` interface), and consequently, be able to answer two questions:

- Do I have any more elements?

- If so, what is that element?

JavaScript announced similar support for objects and collections to be made iterable in ES6. However, JavaScript being an interpreted language has no runtime enforcement of a contract, rather, JavaScript imposes the behavior via convention. This convention is as follows—for any object to be iterable, it must have a method name that evaluates to `Symbol.iterator` (yet another well-known symbol). The return value of this method **must** be an object that has a zero arity (i.e., no arguments) `next` method, which in turn returns an object with two properties:

- `done`—a boolean that answers whether there are any more elements that could be iterated upon

- `value`—the current item

We can make things a little clearer with a simple example:

```
const arrayList = { ①
  data: [1, 2, 3, 4, 5],
  [Symbol.iterator]() { ②
```

```
    let index = 0;
    return { ③
      next: () => { ④
        if (index === this.data.length) {
          return {
            done: true, ⑤
          };
        }
        const ret = this.data[index];
        index++;
        return {
          done: false,
          value: ret,
        }; ⑥
      },
    };
  },
};
const iterator = arrayList[Symbol.iterator](); ⑦
// prints '{ done: false, value: 1 }'
console.log(iterator.next()); ⑧
```

① Define a simple object

② Implement the Symbol.iterator method

③ The iterator method returns the iterable

④ The iterable implements the next method

⑤ If we are done iterating signal done as true

⑥ If we are not done, return the value

⑦ Grab a reference to the iterator

⑧ Start iterating

We make an attempt to implement an iterable arraylist here. Since we are to adhere to the iterability protocol, we implement a method with the name `Symbol.iterator`. The iterator method, when invoked, returns a new object that performs the iteration for us.

Note that the return value of any invocation on `next` returns an object that appropriatcly has the `done` flag set, as well as the `value` if needed.

Now that we have a handle on what an implementation might look like, let us tease apart the moving parts. Iteration in JavaScript consists of two (or three depending on how you look at it) different pieces:

- The object that is "iterable," that is, the object that has the `Symbol.iterator` method

- The object that is *returned* from invoking the iterator method, the "iterator" which in turn has the `next` method on it

Finally, there is the result of the next invocation, which we may consider as part of the iterator contract, or simply the iterator result. We are done! Our `arrayList` successfully implements all the pieces needed to make it iterable. Now, we can make use of the `for-of` loop to iterate over it, just like we can with arrays. Observe:

```
// use the arrayList implementation from our earlier example
for (const v of arrayList) {
  // prints // 1, 2, 3, 4, 5 in sequence
  console.log(v);
}
```

All this boils down to JavaScript now having a canonical API that any client can safely use to iterate over our objects!

## Cleaning Up

We know that iterators need implement the `next` method. This method, upon reaching the end of the iterable object, can do any cleanup that is necessary, just prior to signaling the end via `{ done: true }`.

However, what happens if the consumer were to stop the iteration prematurely? Well, iterators can (optionally) implement a `return` method, which will be invoked if the consumer terminates the iteration. Consider the following:

```
const incrementor = {
  [Symbol.iterator]() {
    let start = 0;
    return {
      next() {
        return {
          value: start++,
          done: false,
        };
      },
      return: function () { ①
        console.log('Cleaning up ...');
        return {
          done: true,
        };
      },
    };
  },
};

for (const v of incrementor) {
  if (v > 10) {
    break; ②
  }
  console.log(v);
}
```

① Implement both the required `next` and optional `return` method

② Break out prematurely in a `for-of` loop

Here we have a simple incrementing iterable that happens to implement both the next and the `return` method. We use our new friend, the `for-of` loop to start iterating over our object, and conditionally break out of the loop. If we were to run this example, we will see the cleaning message show in our console. Notice that we return a `done: true` to signal that the iterator is now done.

This mechanism is a side effect of the `for-of` loop knowing the iterator machinery—furthermore, it's not only `break`, but `throw`-ing an error *inside* the `for-loop` as well as `return`-ing from within a `for-loop` that will invoke the iterator's `return` method.

If we were invoking the `next` method explicitly, then it is required that we call `return` when we are done.

## Other Benefits

Having a standard approach to iterability permits JavaScript to build additional constructs on top of the API, while simultaneously allowing other libraries to devise their objects to leverage the same mechanisms. In Chapter 4 we discussed the `spread` operator, and learned that anything that is iterable is also spreadable. Reiterating, the spread operator introduced in ES6 hooks into the exact same machinery that the `for-of` loop does.

Furthermore, going forward, any object, including ones that we may introduce in our applications, the collections provided by libraries like `Immutable.js` as well as `NodeLists` (returned by `document.querySelectorAll`) can be both safely and correctly looped over, as well as "spread"![3]

Finally, and this is subtle, we introduce a mechanism to allow for lazy evaluation of code! An iterable object gives the consumer back an iterator, and simply waits for the iterator's `next` method to be invoked. If and when the `next` method is invoked, the object can then calculate (if necessary) the next item in the sequence, and return it! Take that a step further, our iterables could also be infinite (within the bounds of overflow of course).

We have discussed the iterable, and the iteration protocol in this section. Next, we will take a look at "pausable" functions, and some use-cases.

---

[3]Turns out, all the collections offered by immutable.js as well the NodeList are iterables.

# Generators

Generator functions are a new addition in ES6 that introduce new syntax and keywords, as well as new semantics for functions. Let us first take a look at a simple example and then we will proceed to see how it works:

*Defining a simple generator*

```
function* generatorDemo() {
  yield 10;
  console.log('First time');
  yield 20;
  console.log('Second time');
}

const generator = generatorDemo(); // prints nothing to the log
console.assert(generator !== undefined);

// following each line is what you see in the console
console.log(generator.next());
// { value: 10, done: false }
console.log(generator.next());
// First time
// { value: 20, done: false }
console.log(generator.next());
// Second time
// { value: undefined, done: true }

// alternatively, we can just use the for-of loop
for (const i of generatorDemo()) {
  console.log(i);
}
```

Let us focus on the syntactic aspects here—we are introduced to the new function* (i.e., *not* a typo), as well a new yield keyword.

When we invoke the generator function, we see two interesting things happen—we see nothing in the console (if this were a regular function, we would expect to see our console.log statement print out our messages), and we get *something back* from as a return value!

See, when a generator function is invoked, it immediately returns a generator object **without** executing its body. Furthermore, if we are to observe the proceeding lines in our example, we see that this returned object has a next method on it, which in turn, returns another object with value and done keys in it. In other words, the generator object is iterable!

What role does yield perform? If we look closely at the output of our example code, we notice that upon invoking next on the iterator, the body of the generator function is executed only up until the first yield statement is encountered, at which time, whatever value is "yielded" is returned to the invoking code (wrapped in an iterator result object). In effect, the yield statement *suspends* the execution of the generator function, returning control to the invocation context.

An analogy that works is one of ping-pong (or tennis) with two players. Once we initiate the play (i.e., we have the generator object in our hands), invoking next sends control over to the generator function's court. Upon a yield, the generator returns control to the invokee with a value. We, the "consumer" can choose to stop playing by not invoking next again at which point the generator function (if it is not "done" yet remains in a suspended state), and the generator will end the play if it reaches the end of its body's definition (at which point the value returned is {done: true}).

In essence, a generator function is a function that returns an iterable object, which in turn implements the iterator protocol. A generator function pauses (using yield), and resumes when the invokee invokes next.

Let us convert our Fibonacci example to use a generator function:

```
function* fibonacci() {
  let start = 0;
  let next = 1;
  yield start;
  yield next;
  while (true) {
    const result = start + next;
    start = next;
    next = result;
    yield result;
  }
}
```

```
const f = fibonacci();
console.log(f.next().value); // 0
console.log(f.next().value); // 1
console.log(f.next().value); // 1
console.log(f.next().value); // 2
console.log(f.next().value); // 3
console.log(f.next().value); // 5
console.log(f.next().value); // 8
```

This implementation isn't that much different from our earlier implementation using `Symbol.iterator`, except we no longer need to implement that method—the generator function does it all for us.

## Generators as Consumers

Our exploration of generators so far has seen them as data "producers"—they yield values per iteration. Generators, despite their name, can also act as "consumers," wherein we can "push" values onto them, perhaps as a seed, or a way to send data to them for them to use.

Let us tweak our simplistic example and see how this plays out:

```
function* generatorWithPushDemo() {
  const first = yield 10;
  console.log('First time', first);
  const second = yield 20;
  console.log('Second time', second);
}

const generator = generatorWithPushDemo(); // prints nothing to the log
console.assert(generator !== undefined);

// following each line is what you see in the console
console.log(generator.next()); ①
// { value: 10, done: false }
console.log(generator.next('sending a value in')); ②
// First time sending a value in
// { value: 20, done: false }
```

```
console.log(generator.next('sending another value in')); ③
// Second time sending another value in
// { value: undefined, done: true }
```

① Kick off the iteration with a `next`

② Push a value as an argument to the `next` method, effectively setting the value of `first`

③ Do the same again, except this time set the value of `second`

We start with getting a reference to the generator object, then invoke `next`. Control goes to the generator, and it `yields` a value back to us. At this point, the generator is suspended.

This is where things get interesting—we invoke `next` again, except this time we supply an argument. This value is *assigned* to the `first` variable, and the generator can now use this value within its implementation. One way to think about this is that any value we pass *into* the generator effectively replaces the `yield` in the generator. Of course, if the yield statement was not being captured within the generator, passing values in the generator results in a no-op—the value passed in is simply ignored.

## Cleaning Up

Custom iterators can implement a `return` method that can be used to clean up if the consumer terminates the iteration prematurely (using `break`, `throw,` or `return`). It turns out that the generator object returned by generator functions can do the same.

But wait, you say, we don't implement the `next` method! If the caller were to invoke `return`, how are we, the generator function authors, supposed to clean up?

Well, it turns out, JavaScript already has a cleanup mechanism—it's the `try-catch-finally` block! Here is how it works—if our generator implementation were to have a try block, and the caller were to invoke `return` on the resultant generator, JavaScript will execute the `finally` block within the generator function for us:

```
function* generatorFunctionWithTryCatchFinally() {
  try { ①
    console.log('Started');
    yield 'some value';
  } catch (error) {
```

```
    console.log('Caught: ' + error);
  } finally {
    console.log('Finally block');
  }
}

const callee = generatorFunctionWithTryCatchFinally();
console.log(callee.next());
// Started
// { value: 'some value', done: false }
console.log(callee.return());  ②
// Finally block
// { value: undefined, done: true }

console.log('----------');

for (const looped of generatorFunctionWithTryCatchFinally()) {  ③
  console.log(looped);
  // Started
  // some value
  // Finally block
}

console.log('----------');

const c = generatorFunctionWithTryCatchFinally();
console.log(c.next());
// Started
// { value: 'some value', done: false }
console.log(c.throw(new Error('Stop now!')));  ④
// Caught: Error: Stop now!
// Finally block
// { value: undefined, done: true }
```

① Wrap the body of the generator in a try block

② Invoke the return method on the generator

③ Use the native `for-of` loop to drive the generator to completion

④ Use the `throw` method to case the generator to error out and stop

We write a simple generator that has its body wrapped in a `try-catch-finally` block. We grab a reference to the generator object, and invoke `return` on it. The example enumerates the output we see in the console, and we see that the `finally` block is executed for us at this time.

Our next attempt uses the `for-of` loop to get a reference to the generator and drive it to completion. Again, if we are to observe the output, we see that the `finally` block of the generator function is invoked at the end. In other words, the `for-of` loop automatically invokes the `return` method of the generator, just like we saw in the case of custom iterators.

Finally, there happens to be yet another method that generator objects implement, namely `throw`. Going back to the table-tennis analogy, rather than sending the ball (a value) into the generator, we are throwing at error at it. Much like sending a value (using `next(someValue)`) replaces the yield statement *inside* the generator, `throw`-ing an error causes the generator to throw that error at the place where it was suspended. If there were no try-catch block around that line, then the generator function would simply report the error at that line. In our example, however, we *do* have a try-catch, and appropriately, the `catch` block is executed, followed by the `finally` block.

As we can see in this example, generator functions, and the resulting generator objects give us the same capabilities as iterators do, maintaining the symmetry between custom iterators and automatically produced ones. The only exception here is that generator objects also implement the `throw` method, which does not apply to other iterables.

# Other Benefits

Generators allow us to write lazily evaluated code, as well as have the ability to produce infinite sequences, both of which we see embodied in our Fibonacci sequence generator. Leaving aside all the machinery of generators, we must always remember that they produce iterators. Many functions that we write tend to return sequences, like arrays, except we are forced to populate the array upfront, regardless of what the client might need to do with it. Generators give us a mechanism for clients to proactively ask for items, thus potentially optimizing how much work needs done.

We must always bear in mind that generator functions, with the idea of suspending and resuming, are a great fit for any situation where we see transfer of control from one context to another, and back. One obvious candidate is asynchronous operations, where control goes back and forth from the main execution context, to a callback, and back.

## Additional Syntactic Considerations

Consider a scenario in which one generator function (we will call this "outer") invokes another generator function (called "inner") as part of its implementation. Given that our intent is to consume all the yield-ed values of both the outer and the inner generator functions, we need an additional mechanism to suspend the outer generator, loop over all of the inner generator's yielded values, and then return control back to the outer generator thereby resuming it. This is where a new keyword, namely yield*, comes into play. Consider the following:

```
function* inner() { ①
  yield 'b';
  yield 'c';
  yield 'd';
}

function* outer() { ②
  yield 'a';
  console.log('after the first outer yield');
  yield* inner(); ③
  console.log('after finishing the inner yield*');
  yield 'e';
}

for (const v of outer()) {
  console.log(v);
}
// a
// after the first outer yield
// b
```

```
// c
// d
// after finishing the inner yield*
// e
```

      ① Our so-called inner generator function

      ② Our main or "outer" generator function

      ③ Using the `yield*` expression to invoke the inner generator and drive it to completion

We start with two generator functions, except that the outer one delegates to the inner one using `yield*`. We see from the output that the outer generator first yields a value, then upon a `next` (via the `for-loop`), hands control over to the inner generator, and when (if) it is done, resumes the outer generator.

A subtle aspect about `yield*` is that it is given the *result* of invoking the inner generator (via `inner()`) and **not** a reference to it (i.e., `inner`). In other words, it is given a generator object over which it can loop. It turns out that `yield*` can be given *any* iterable—a generator object, an array, map, set, string, or even a custom iterable that we handcrafted. Bear in mind though that while **all** of these implement the `next` and `return` method, only generator objects implement the `throw` method.

## Summary

In this chapter, we saw how JavaScript now offers a standard mechanism for iteration, making it possible for consumers and producers of sequences to adhere to a canonical API for iteration. We also saw how generator functions and objects allow us to write lazy code, and generate infinite sequences. While it may seem that the machinery surrounding generators is complex, it will serve to remember the symmetry that iterables and generators offer—they happen to be two sides of the same coin.

In the next chapter, we will explore the new promise API, which, thanks to ES6, is supported natively in JavaScript. We will see how we can wrap legacy callback-based APIs using promises, allowing us to embrace promises everywhere.

# CHAPTER 10

# Avoiding Callbacks with Promises

Working with asynchronous operations is tedious. For the longest time we resorted to using callbacks which proved hard to get right especially when it came to state management and error propagation. We then elevated the abstraction, leveraging promises. However, those too came with their own set of problems—with different libraries having varying implementations, leaving us frustrated and looking for a sane way to grapple with asynchronous operations.

That changes now! JavaScript introduces promises in ES6 as a native API, elevating promises to be a first-class citizen in the language. In this chapter we will explore the API that promises offer, so that we can start using promises in our code, doing away with callbacks. We will also learn how we can wrap operations that intrinsically assume a callback, so that we can consistently use promises everywhere. Given what we will learn in this chapter, we will once and for all get rid of callbacks, while making our code easier to write and reason about.

## The Broken Promises of Promises

JavaScript is, by design, a language that enforces an asynchronous programming paradigm. As JavaScript developers, we are well versed in the fact that our code runs in a single thread. Therefore, "blocking" operations—I/O, network requests, and even periodic invocations (using `setInterval`)—all need to be performed asynchronously. That is, they need to be performed in a way that does **not** block the main thread.

Idiomatically, this is accomplished using callbacks. Asynchronous APIs expect one, or more "handler" functions as arguments, and these handlers are invoked with the result (or error) of the asynchronous call. The handler encompasses what to do if and when the asynchronous call finishes.

© Raju Gandhi 2019
R. Gandhi, *JavaScript Next*, https://doi.org/10.1007/978-1-4842-5394-6_10

Callbacks, while idiomatic, can prove to be hard to work with. Attempts at sequencing asynchronous calls (where the invocation of one relies on the response of a previous call) can lead to nested callbacks (affectionately referred to as the pyramid of doom[1]). This nested code style leads to higher coupling, making it harder to test. Since the handler runs in a different "context" from the rest of your code, error reporting and propagation require careful handling and management.

Callbacks enforce an eager programming style, in that, any asynchronous function that expects a callback as an argument forces the client to know exactly what needs done *before* the operation completes. Since the callback **has** to be defined prior to invoking the asynchronous operation, one cannot defer *how* we consume the result of the call to *after* having started, or finished the work. Conceptually, the (asynchronous) task to be performed is tied to the work that will be done after the task finishes.

But most importantly, reading code involving callbacks involves some mental gymnastics, and makes it hard to reason about the code, even more so when the callbacks are nested within one another. Granted, we could refactor our callbacks to be standalone functions, and use those instead, but that seems akin to kicking the can down the road. There have been several strategies used when working with nested callbacks, many of which have been captured in web sites like Callback Hell.[2]

So came along promises. As the name suggests, a promise represents the result of some work that is to happen *eventually*. When using promises, asynchronous calls, rather than accepting a handler, immediately return a promise object (or are wrapped in one). This promise, which represents the result of a potential success/failure *in the future*, can then be passed around to other pieces of your application, elevating the notion of asynchronous work to being a first-class citizen just like any other object.

This promise "token" exposes a then method, which expects another handler, and in turn returns a new promise that wraps the result of that handler in a promise. The handler supplied to then is the work that is to be done when the promise it is chained to completes. This allows us to *defer* what we wish to do with the result of an asynchronous operation till later, in effect, decoupling where we start the work, from where we consume the results.

Considering the then API itself returns a promise permits us to "chain" promises, thus providing us with a mechanism to eloquently express sequencing—in effect, "Do this, when it is done, *then* do this."

---

[1]https://en.wikipedia.org/wiki/Pyramid_of_doom_(programming)
[2]http://callbackhell.com/

Finally, a promise object exposes a mechanism to trap any errors, usually with a `catch` method, and this allows for trapping, and dealing with any errors that might occur, anywhere in the promise chain.

Promises are a simple abstraction on top of callbacks—they simply provide a mechanism to wrap callbacks, alleviating the need for us developers to deal with state and error management.

However, for so long, promises were implemented as a library. Popular stand-along implementations include Kris Kowal's q[3] and libraries like jQuery shipped with their own internal implementations. Developers who wished to use promises were either forced to include (explicitly or implicitly) a third-party library since the language had no support for the same.

This leads to the second point—while there exists a community-driven specification[4] to dictate how JavaScript promises are to work, there was no guarantee that an implementation *actually* adhered to the specification, or how true (to the specification) the implementation was. In other words, there was no canonical API to work with promises that made clients agnostic of the implementation details.

Add to that the fact that many libraries and frameworks chose to adhere to native language constructs (of which there is only one—the callback), thus creating a schism, where often code, in one application used both callbacks and promises, furthering the confusion.

To address these issues, ES6 introduces the promise API to JavaScript. Let us dive into the details of this API next.

## Using Promises

Promises are created using the `Promise` constructor, which takes as its sole argument a single function. This function, in turn, receives two arguments, wherein both arguments happen to functions themselves. The first argument provides the means to signal a successful resolution of the promise, while the second signals a failed resolution. Let us consider a simple example to make this idea concrete:

```
const shouldResolve = true;
const p = new Promise((resolve, reject) => { ①
```

---

[3]https://github.com/kriskowal/q
[4]https://promisesaplus.com/

```
  if (shouldResolve) {
    resolve('I transitioned successfully'); ②
  } else {
    reject(new Error('I failed to resolve')); ③
  }
});
console.log(p);
```

① Create a promise using the constructor

② resolve it conditionally

③ Else reject it

We introduce *some* conditional as mechanism to mimic a real-world scenario where the promise might successfully resolve, or fail to do so. To follow the happy path (initially), we set the conditional to true. We then proceed to create a promise using the constructor, conditionally "resolve"-ing with a message by invoking the first argument to the callback handler, aptly named resolve. If we were to run this in our browser console, we see the following:

```
Promise { <state>: "fulfilled", <value>: "I transitioned successfully" }
```

Since our conditional allowed the promise to be "resolve"-ed, the promise now in a "fulfilled" state reports our success message.

If we were to try running the same snippet with the conditional set to false, we notice the promise was "rejected."

```
Promise { <state>: "rejected" }
```

The promise constructor provides a mechanism to wrap any existing functions or operations that perform asynchronous tasks. Many legacy APIs expect a callback; however, if we wish to use promises everywhere (which we should), it's easy to hide this from consumers going forward, like so:

```
const asyncRequest = (method, url) => ①
  new Promise((resolve, reject) => {
    const xhr = new XMLHttpRequest();
    xhr.open(method, url, true);
    xhr.onload = () => resolve(xhr.response); ②
```

```
    xhr.onerror = () => reject(new Error(xhr.statusText)); ③
    xhr.send();
  });
```

```
const req1 = asyncRequest('GET', 'https://my-json-server.typicode.com/
typicode/demo/posts');
```

① Wrap a `XMLHttpRequest` call in a function

② If the request succeeds, `resolve` the promise with the response from `XMLHttpRequest` object

③ Else `reject` it, appropriately wrapping the response

We attempt to (rather naively[5] I must admit) wrap requests using `XMLHttpRequest` in a promise API. Now, any call to `request` simply returns a promise, that is, in this instance `req` is a `Promise` object.

As one might surmise, a promise acts like a state machine. Once constructed, a promise is in "pending" state, and eventually "transitions" to either being "fulfilled," if it is resolved, or to a "reject"-ed state, if it is rejected, lending the state of the promise to "settled." Once settled, a promise **cannot** revert to any of its previous states, nor can it transition to any other state.

Onto the promise API!

## Using Promises

The Promises/A+ specification alludes to a `thenable` object, which is an object that acts like a promise, and happens to have a `then` method. ES6 promises are Promises/A+ compliant, and correspondingly expose a `then` method that allows clients to access the *eventual* result of a resolved promise, or the reason for it being rejected.

An interested party can express interest in the value of the promise *at any time* (even after the promise has transitioned) by attaching a handler to its `then` method. This callback will be invoked if the promise resolves successfully.

---

[5]This implementation has a few shortcomings. It instantiates the `XMLHttpRequest` internally, thus preventing the client from configuring the actual request. Secondly, it only `rejects` the promise if the request *fails*, not if the response contains a non-200 status.

The then method can also take a second, optional argument which is the error callback, and this callback will be invoked if the promise were to be rejected; however, this is considered to be an anti-pattern.[6] In order to catch errors in the promise chain, promise objects also expose a catch method, which will trap any rejected cases. finally is yet another method that promises expose, that allow us to do any cleanup once the promise is settled; in other words, the handler supplied to finally will be invoked regardless of the promise being resolved or rejected.

then, catch, and finally are all guaranteed to return promise objects. That is, we are not required to wrap the return value of these callbacks in promises—we can simply return any value or reference, and the underlying machinery will automatically wrap the return value in a promise for us.

Thus, idiomatically, resolve and then method *should,* respectively, capture and return values, allowing consumers downstream to continue chaining, while reject-ion should be done using an Error object, which captures a stacktrace thus making debugging a lot easier.

Which begs the question—what should the return value of catch be? Recall that both then and catch return promises—so if there is a way to recover from an error, and allow for continuation of the promise chain, then a catch handler can return a value while simultaneously allowing for side effects (such as logging the error)! This allows consumers downstream to remain agnostic of errors, and may continue chaining knowing that they will get a value, albeit a default of some sort.

finally is a bit of an exception—it takes no arguments, and is simply a mechanism that allows for any cleanup required after the promise resolves. The finally block **will** be invoked regardless of a resolution or a rejection, much like any try-catch-finally block you might be used to in other languages.

A quick demonstration is in order. We will build upon our promisified XMLHttpRequest example, and register appropriate listeners for a result, and trap any errors.

```
const req1 = asyncRequest('GET', 'https://my-json-server.typicode.com/
typicode/demo/posts');
req1
  .then(json => JSON.parse(json)) ①
  .then(resp => resp.map(item => item.id))
```

---

[6]https://stackoverflow.com/a/30882722

```
.then((ids) => {
  console.log(`Found ${ids.length} posts`);
  return ids;
})
.catch(err => console.log(err)); ②
```

① Attach several handlers using the then method

② Ensure we trap any errors using catch

The promise API, outside of being fluent, provides a very elegant mechanism to decouple *starting* an asynchronous operation, from the consumption of the results of said operation. Gone are the nested callbacks; instead the multiple thens allow us to (better) align our code with how we think and reason about our programs. Furthermore, since the chain correctly propagates errors, we can safely trap *any* error that may occur in the promise chain.

## All or Nothing

There are scenarios in which we wish to start a multitude of (asynchronous) operations in parallel, treating them either as a collective "whole," insofar that we care about all of the resolved values, or just one. This is different than us attempting to sequence operations, which is when we would use the then method available on promises.

The promise API exposes two class level methods, namely all and race which attempt to fulfill this requirement.

Consider a scenario where you wish to read from multiple files (on disk), or gather information from a slew of different endpoints, and only after all the requests complete, collate the results. We can use Promise.all to start up multiple concurrent requests and wait for all of them to complete, like so:

```
const p = asyncRequest('GET', 'https://my-json-server.typicode.com/
typicode/demo/posts'); ①
const c = asyncRequest('GET', 'https://my-json-server.typicode.com/
typicode/demo/comments'); ②

Promise.all([p, c]) ③
  .then(([posts, comments]) => ({ ④
    posts: JSON.parse(posts),
```

```
    comments: JSON.parse(comments),
  }))
  .then(obj => console.log(obj))
  .catch(err => console.log(err));
```

① Start a lookup for all of a user's posts

② Similarly one for all comments

③ Use `all` to start multiple operations in parallel

④ Receive an array of resolved values in the same order as the supplied promises

We care to fetch all of the posts and the comments for a particular user, which are independent requests. `Promise.all` takes an array of promises, and in turn, returns a promise. If and only if all of the promises supplied to `all` resolve, it collects all of the fulfilled values into an array, ordering them in the same order as the original order of promises, and calls our `then` handler.

However, if one or more promises were to fail (with a rejection or an error), then the promise that `all` returns is rejected as well.

Alternatively, there is `Promise.race`. As the name suggests, given an array of promises, the first promise to resolve wins the race (or the first one to be rejected), and the resolved value of the "winning" promise is the single argument supplied to the handler (thus discarding the results of any other promises that resolve afterward).

One interesting use-case for `Promise.race` is when we wish to timeout an asynchronous operation, like so:

```
const p = asyncRequest('GET', 'https://my-json-server.typicode.com/
typicode/demo/posts'); ①
const timer = new Promise((_, reject) => setTimeout(reject, 1000)); ②

Promise.race([p, timer]) ③
  .then(posts => ({ ④
    posts: JSON.parse(posts),
  }))
  .catch(() => ({ ⑤
    posts: [],
  }))
  .then(obj => console.log(obj));
```

① Start a lookup for all of a user's posts

② Wrap `setTimeout` in a promise that is rejected after the set interval

③ Use `race` to start multiple operations in parallel

④ Receive the array of posts if our request completes prior to our timeout

⑤ Else catch the rejection to compose a default return value for subsequent consumers

We leverage multiple techniques here—(naively) wrapping an asynchronous operation like `setTimeout` in a promise, `race`-ing our actual request against one that is rejected on a timeout, and returning defaults from a `catch` method so subsequent consumers can continue chaining.[7] If you wish to see how `race` behaves if we were to timeout before our Ajax request is resolved, simply lower the timeout limit to perhaps `ten`.

Finally, the promise API exposes two additional (static) methods, namely `Promise.resolve` and `Promise.reject` which act as handy shortcuts, particularly when testing.

# Caveats

The first limitation is that promises are eager, in that once we initiate an operation using a promise, that work **will** be performed, regardless of whether there is an interested consumer. That is, a promise will attempt to carry out its assigned duties without waiting for a client to attach a `then` handler.

Consider a scenario where you attempt to resolve some data (via an Ajax call) that is to be displayed in a widget prior to displaying the widget on the screen. Now, let's say that a user interaction causes it so that the widget is no longer needed. Since promises are eager, the process that fetches the data happens regardless of whether there is a widget to consume them. *If* the promise were to wait till the widget attached a `then` handler, then our worries would be over. But alas!

In addition to promises being eager (or *not* lazy), they are also not cancelable. That is, the promise object does not expose an API to cancel the underlying process that it wraps. Consider a search interface that attempts to refresh the results displayed as we type our query (much like Google's or Netflix's). This requires that we make an Ajax call

---

[7]This **will** depend on your use-case, but it is certainly a technique worthy of remembering.

to the backend for every character typed. However, there is a good chance that we start a backend call based on the characters in the search input box, and depending on how fast the user types, we may have to start another query before the previous one completes. It would be nice if we could simply cancel the previous query prior to starting a new one.

All of this boils down to one simple rule of thumb—don't compose a promise unless you are sure you are going to use it!

# The Benefits of a Native API

The fact that the promise API is now part of the language offers a **huge** advantage over using a library, which is, we now have a standard API that unifies how browser vendors, libraries, and frameworks can wrap asynchronous operations. For example, `window.fetch`[8] can now return a promise, because the language now natively supports promises. One side effect of this is now we have one vocabulary to work with anything asynchronous, allowing us, the developers, to develop a richer set of patterns and anti-patterns that rally around one central construct, namely the promise. Correspondingly, other language constructs like `async/await`, which we will discuss soon, can also safely use promises.

More so, the introduction of the promise API in JavaScript is in line with other features we have seen, like iterables, that attempt to provide a common denominator for both library/framework writers and consumers, while not diverging away from well-established community standards like the Promises/A+ specification.

Going forward, we, as JavaScript developers, will benefit if we rally around (native) promises, be that in our code or in the expectations we set from the libraries and frameworks we use. Of course, if nothing else, we might be able to finally shed our dependency on yet another third-party library. :)

---

[8]https://developer.mozilla.org/en-US/docs/Web/API/WindowOrWorkerGlobalScope/fetch

# Summary

Promises, offered as a native API in JavaScript offer a significant advantage over using third-party libraries, by allowing all asynchronous operations, be that native or other, to return a promise. Granted that promises come with their own concerns, however, they are a huge leap forward from the world we previously inhabited, wherein we had inconsistent semantics when working with asynchronous operations.

In the next chapter we will look at a much-wanted language feature, namely the ability to declare classes to build inheritance trees in JavaScript.

# CHAPTER 11

# Many of a Kind with Classes

Building objects via classes, and organizing them in hierarchies in JavaScript, is hard. Functions, constructors, the prototype property—combine all of these using a secret recipe, sprinkle some magic dust, and voila, we have inheritance, *assuming* we get all the wiring correct. Without having an intricate understanding of how JavaScript prototypal inheritance works, it feels like its black magic.

In this chapter we will see how we can easily create classes and build inheritance trees in our code using several new keywords like `class`, `extends,` and `super` that were introduced in ES6, allowing us to express our intent just as we would have in other object-oriented languages. Once we are done with this chapter, we will be confident in our abilities to model our problem space comprehensibly. We will also walk away with a nuanced view of when we should reach for this new feature in our codebase, and times when we might be better off without it.

## The Difficulties of Building Classes and Inheritance in JavaScript

JavaScript is object-oriented, where objects can act as "bags" of data, and methods, which happen to be functions that can operate on the contained data. JavaScript embodies prototypal inheritance, wherein objects extend from other objects, which, when coupled with its dynamic typing, is arguably much more powerful than classical inheritance seen in languages like Java or C#. Granted, JavaScript does not seem to lend itself to principles that are obvious in other languages like abstraction, polymorphism, inheritance, and encapsulation—however, with a little bit of trickery, many of these *can* be achieved.

© Raju Gandhi 2019

R. Gandhi, *JavaScript Next*, https://doi.org/10.1007/978-1-4842-5394-6_11

And herein lies the rub—while many of the aforementioned object-oriented facets *are* possible in JavaScript, it is extremely hard to get right without having intimate knowledge of everything involved to make the magic happen. One needs to understand how functions can act as constructors, how new-ing creates objects, and how the constructor invocation wires up the resulting objects prototype. It also requires one to grok how the `constructor` and `prototype` property work within the instance to allow for things like inheritance to work. Consider the following snippet:

```
function Person(name) { ①
  this.name = name;
}

Person.prototype.getName = function () { ②
  return this.name;
};

Person.prototype.sayHello = function (to) { ③
  return `Hello ${to.getName()}. My name is ${this.name}.`;
};

const raju = new Person('Raju');
const venkat = new Person('Venkat');

// prints 'Hello Venkat. My name is Raju'
console.log(raju.sayHello(venkat));
```

        ① A constructor function

        ② Tack on an instance method on the function's prototype

        ③ Add another instance method

Let us break it apart, one piece at a time. Before we start, bear in mind that functions in JavaScript *are* objects, and like objects, can have properties. One such property happens to be the `prototype` property.

In our example, we leverage the fact that functions play a dual role in JavaScript. That is, they can act both as regular functions, and constructors, much like constructors we may be used to in other languages like Java or C#. The only difference between a regular function invocation and constructor function invocation is that the latter uses the new keyword.

When a function is invoked with the new keyword, a new object is created that has a hidden pointer to the prototype of the function that created it, and this is bound to this new object inside the body of the constructor function. In other words, anytime we use this *inside* the body of a (constructor) function, we are referring to this new object, that happens to be an "instance" created by that function.

Consequently, any time we tack on a property, like this.name we are simply tacking it on the *newly created instance.* However, if we wish to have "instance" methods for all instances created by a function, then we leverage the fact that the newly created object has a pointer to the functions prototype, so by saying Person.prototype we are changing the prototype of the new object!

Finally, since all instances of this function have the same methods (since they belong to the shared prototype object), we can invoke one instance method from another, for example, we can use getName from sayHello.

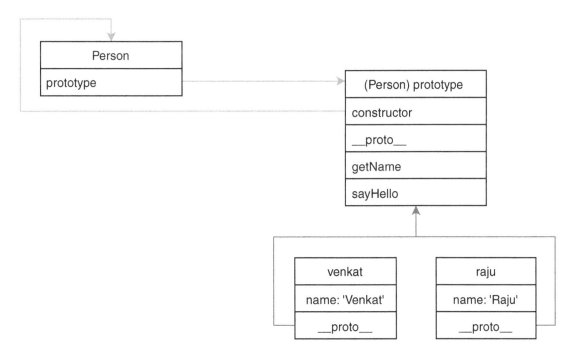

***Figure 11-1.*** *Prototypal inheritance*

This picture describes how prototypal inheritance works, wherein, the newly created instance references the prototype of the function that created it.[1] If we are to look up a property (or invoke a method) that does not exist on the instance itself, then the object *delegates* to its prototype, thus "climbing" the inheritance tree. Of course, if we reach the end of the prototype chain, and the property was not found, we would get an undefined.

The thing to bear in mind about the prototype object is that it is *just* a POJO—a plain old JavaScript object! It is no different that if we had created an object using the object literal ({}). This is precisely why it's referred to as "prototypal" inheritance—one object acts as the prototype of another—objects inherit from other objects.

Along the same vein, by default, all objects inherently inherit from Object. prototype.[2] This rule applies to any object we create using {} as well as to the prototype objects that are attached by JavaScript to functions objects.

To complete the picture, Object.prototype has a few methods tacked onto it, like toString. Keeping all this in mind, our all-pictorial representation of this becomes what is shown in Figure 11-2.

---

[1]In this diagram, the __proto__ property is represented as the hidden pointer to the objects prototype. While this property does exist in some implementation, it is one we **cannot** assume. If we wish to get the prototype of any object, we should use the Object.getPrototypeOf method.

[2]This object, like any function's prototype object, is simply another POJO.

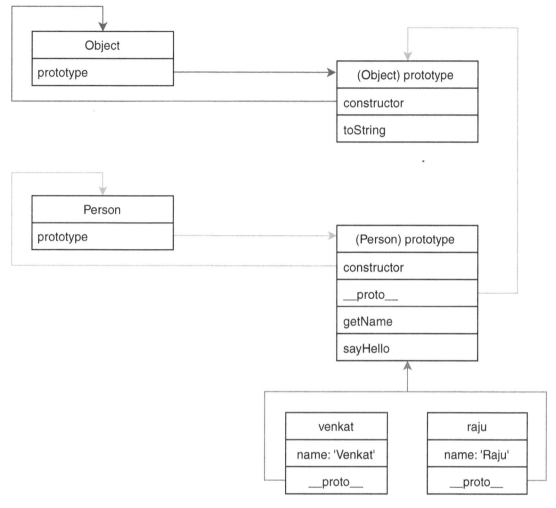

***Figure 11-2.*** *Inheriting from* `Object`

Extending our previous discussion, if we were to call `toString` on an instance of `Person`, JavaScript would start with the instance, realize it does not have that method, follow the prototype chain up to the it's prototype, and continue to do so till it reaches `Object.prototype`, and invoke that method.

We are already seeing the glimmer of how prototypal inheritance works in JavaScript. But how do we create an inheritance hierarchy like we would in other languages? Let us take see how we "extend" from our earlier implementation of `Person` to create a `SuperHero`:

```
function SuperHero(name, superpower) { ①
  // super call - can pass args
  Person.call(this, name); ②
  this.superpower = superpower;
}

SuperHero.prototype = Object.create(Person.prototype); ③

SuperHero.prototype.warCry = function () { ④
  return `My name is ${this.name}!!!`;
};

SuperHero.prototype.constructor = SuperHero; ⑤

const thor = new SuperHero('Thor', 'Mjolnir');
// prints 'My name is Thor!!!'
console.log(thor.warCry());
// prints 'Hello Venkat. My name is Thor'
console.log(thor.sayHello(venkat));
```

> ① A "sub-class" constructor
>
> ② We invoke the "super" constructor first
>
> ③ Create the sub-class prototype
>
> ④ Add a method to `SuperHero.prototype`
>
> ⑤ Line up the constructor property of the prototype to point back to the constructor function Phew! A lot of moving parts. However, most of it is simply reproducing what we already know about prototypal inheritance in JavaScript

We start with our implementation of the `Person` constructor, and adding onto `Person.prototype` some instance methods. We then define a `SuperHero` constructor, which is *supposed* to extend `Person`. Inheritance requires that when we invoke the subclass constructor, we first finish constructing our parents (in traditional object-oriented languages this would be a `super` call), and only then continue constructing the subclass instance. How do we emulate this in JavaScript?

Recall that when we invoke a function like a constructor (i.e., invoking it with the new keyword), this inside the constructor definition *is* the newly created instance. In our implementation, we supply this to the Person via the call method available on functions. The call method on function objects forces this inside the callee (in our case Person) to be whatever is supplied as the first argument to call (in our case that is the newly created SuperHero instance).[3] The second argument to call is any arguments that the function expects—in our case that would just be the name. Consequently, the newly created instance gets adorned with whatever the Person constructor tacks on to it, which is exactly what we want.

So, we can emulate a super call. Next item on the menu—align the prototypes correctly. If we were to look back at how prototypal inheritance is implemented, instances point to the prototype of the function that created them. For the whole inheritance tree to work correctly, SuperHero.prototype **must** be an object that points to Person.prototype. Then, and only then, instances of SuperHero will point to SuperHero.prototype, which in turn points to Person.prototype, which by default points to Object.prototype.

It turns out that Object.create can take an object, and returns a new object that uses the supplied object as its prototype. Great! We swap out SuperHero.prototype with the newly created object, then tack on an instance method (which works only for superheroes) on it.

One final detail—since we swapped out the prototype object that JavaScript created for the SuperHero function, we need to wire it so that it knows the function that owns it, so we align the constructor property on SuperHero.prototype to point back to the SuperHero function.[4]

Wow. That is a lot of work to get inheritance working, not to mention how intricate the wiring is, and consequently, how easy it is to miss a step. However, after all that, our pictorial representation transforms to what is shown in Figure 11-3.

---

[3]Contrast this with calling the Person constructor like a function, like Person(). In this case, there is no context; thus this has no meaningful value *inside* the function implementation. In strict mode this inside a function call is actually undefined!

[4]This is how instances of SuperHero can answer the instanceof question—they simply follow their constructor property and see if anyone of their parents are of the type being asked for.

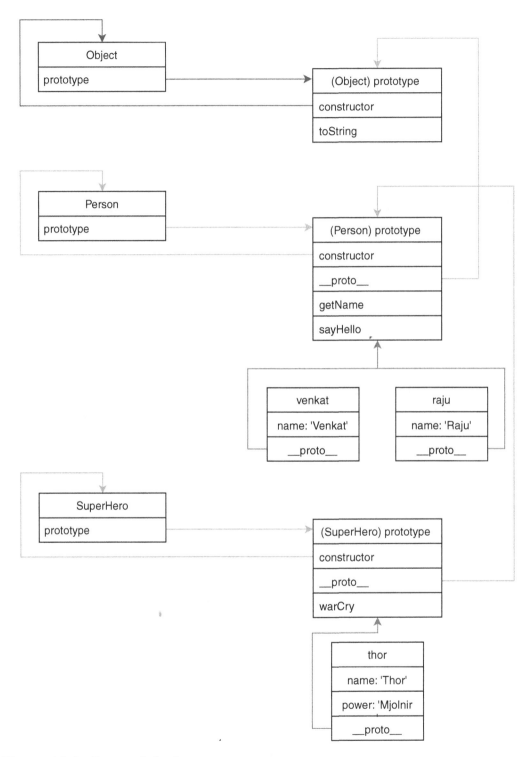

***Figure 11-3.*** *Deeper inheritance*

It is imperative that we realize unlike class-based inheritance, inheritance in JavaScript is achieved via prototypes. Functions act as simple facilitators that allow us to create objects with their prototypes set correctly, thus enabling property and method lookup.

Given that, how does one achieve "static" properties, that is, properties that are associated with the "type" vs. the instance? Simply tack on a property to the object type, which in JavaScript is the function that created that object. So, if we were to tack a property SuperHero.count, we could perhaps keep track of how many superheroes we construct in our application.

As we might conclude, while all of the above is rather elegant, the intent of inheritance *might* be lost in the machinations. Furthermore, the definition of a type is split. Granted, with enough clever code one could attempt to abstract that all to one location, but that does little to alleviate the concern at hand, namely there is already a lot of codes! Is there a better way to realize all this? ES6 activates the class keyword, along with a few others to make all of this a lot easier to work with. Let us take a look.

# Modeling Using Classes

ES6 introduces us to the class keyword, allowing us to express types in a manner that finds parity with other languages. Let us start with simply defining the Person class, and then we will see how inheritance works following that:

```
class Person { ①
  constructor(name) { ②
    this.name = name;
  }

  getName() { ③
    return this.name;
  }

  sayHello(to) { ④
    return `Hello ${to.getName()}. My name is ${this.name}.`;
  }
}
```

```
const raju = new Person('Raju');
const venkat = new Person('Venkat');
// prints 'Hello Venkat. My name is Raju'
console.log(raju.sayHello(venkat));
```

      ① Use the newly activated `class` keyword

      ② Define a constructor for our type

      ③ Define an instance method

      ④ And then another

Right off the bat, a sigh of relief![5]

We introduce a "class" `Person`, with a single-argument constructor. JavaScript requires that if we do *need* a constructor, it must be called `constructor` and we are only allowed to have one constructor per class. However, if our class does not do any work at construction time, then we do not have to write a constructor, and in that case JavaScript will provide us with a default no-argument constructor.

We can also tack on functions to the class like regular methods. JavaScript classes **cannot** have member variables—if we wish to tack on a property on the instance, we must use `this` inside the constructor or any instance method.

Also, all methods in a class, `constructor` included, benefit from many of the features that we have explored—default parameters, destructuring, and spread arguments are all fair game. Using one or more of these features in unison is how we would accomplish overloaded methods for our instances.

As our demonstration shows, the behavior is exactly like we had it working with functions. Onto inheritance!

As we attempted earlier, we want `SuperHero` to inherit from `Person`. Let us see how we can accomplish this using the new syntax:

```
class SuperHero extends Person { ①
  constructor(name, superpower) { ②
    super(name); ③
    this.superpower = superpower;
  }
```

---

[5]Assuming you take my word that this *actually* works :)

```
  warCry() { ④
    return `My name is ${this.name}!!!`;
  }
}

const thor = new SuperHero('Thor', 'Mjolnir');
// prints 'My name is Thor!!!'
console.log(thor.warCry());
// prints 'Hello Venkat. My name is Thor'
console.log(thor.sayHello(venkat));
```

① Use the extends keyword

② Define the constructor

③ Ensure super is invoked

④ Define a SuperHero instance method

In order to extend another class, we simply use the extends keyword, wherein we tell what type we wish to extend. The **first** thing we are **required** to do in the subtype is to invoke super with all of the arguments the parent needs. The rest should be no surprise. Once again, we see that the behavior is no different than what we saw in our function-based implementation.

Classes are allowed to have instance methods like we have seen. They are also allowed to both instance-level and class-level (static) attributes, as well as static methods. However, attributes cannot be introduced inside the class body, and this includes static ones. If we wish to do so, we are forced to define them *outside* the class body.

A static method on the other hand is defined like an instance method except it is prefixed with the static keyword. Such methods can only be accessed on the type, via Classname.staticMethod(). Let us look at an example where we keep track of, and report on the number of superheroes we have constructed:

```
class SuperHero extends Person {
  constructor(name, superpower) {
    super(name);
    this.superpower = superpower;
    SuperHero.internalCount += 1; ①
  }
```

```
  static count() { ②
    return SuperHero.internalCount;
  }
}
SuperHero.internalCount = 0; ③

const thor = new SuperHero('Thor', 'Mjolnir');
const blackWidow = new SuperHero('Black Widow', 'weapons specialist');
// prints 'We have 2 superheroes!'
console.log(`We have ${SuperHero.count()} superheroes!`); ④
```

① Increment the static counter each time the constructor is invoked

② Define a static method that returns the count of superheroes

③ Define an attribute to keep count

④ Invoke the static method

We can reference any static attribute or method by calling them using the class name. However, we have to declare (and in this case initialize) the static property outside the definition of our class. This qualification is also applicable to nonstatic, or instance-level attributes.

Finally, JavaScript does **not** support modifiers, such as `private` or `public`. All attributes and methods defined on a class are public. This again is a departure from traditional languages like Java or C#.

Despite these limitations, I believe we can start to appreciate how this syntax drastically reduces the amount of wiring we have to do by hand, thus reducing any subtle bugs we might introduce when building our own inheritance trees. Admittedly, it feels rather declarative, vs. the imperative modus operandi we adopted when using functions.

Furthermore, to folks coming in from other (class-based) languages, this syntax is very familiar, and thus feels very empowering. This syntax, already in use by frameworks like Angular and libraries like React, makes it far easier for designers to allow mechanisms that allow client code to hook into the life cycle offered by the same.

# Caveats

If the amount of time and effort it takes to explain prototypal inheritance in JavaScript using functions is any measure, then the new syntax wins hands down. Discussing the new syntax almost seems natural, as compared to the extremely intricate and delicate wiring using the old syntax, while accomplishing exactly the same thing.

That said, we are not out of the woods yet. JavaScript has and will continue using prototypal inheritance. The new syntax that ES6 offers is simply syntactic sugar on top of the old! Hence the slightly negative news—we, as JavaScript developers, **must** realize this, and take it upon ourselves to truly understand how prototypal inheritance works under the covers. There is **no** escaping this, and, as JavaScript developers, it behooves us to know how the language really works.

# Summary

JavaScript has always supported the idea of types, as well as inheritance, albeit in a manner that was cumbersome, and one that necessitated an intimate understanding of how (constructor) functions, prototypes, and instances interplayed with one another to make all the magic happen. In this chapter we learned how we can use the new keywords like `class` and `extends` to clearly elucidate what our instances are to look like. We also shined a spotlight on the fact that under the covers this new syntax simply sugars prototypal inheritance, and the pitfalls of always thinking in "object oriented" mode, when perhaps thinking functionally might serve us better.

In the next chapter we will focus on modules that attempt to fill a much-needed gap in JavaScript, namely modules, once and for all doing away with all the schemes we have drummed up to "namespace" our code.

# CHAPTER 12

# Namespacing Code Using Modules

JavaScript's answer to "packaging" or namespacing can be expressed rather succinctly—
it was nonexistent. This has been one of the most glaring omissions in the language
design since the beginning, and has led to a variety of attempts at modularizing code.
These ranged from homegrown solutions to full-blown specifications like AMD.[1]

ES6's answer to this problem is modules. In this chapter we will learn how to
create and consume modules using the new support for the same provided in ES6. We
will be ready to do away with hacky solutions like IEFEs, and be ready to embrace a
consistent, platform agnostic mechanism to encapsulate and namespace our code into
reusable modules. By the end of this chapter, not only will we have a comprehensive
understanding of the nuanced syntax for modules, but also be ready to use the same
with any third-party libraries in our codebase.

## The Lack of Namespacing in JavaScript

In JavaScript, there exists one and only one environment, namely the global scope.
Anything we do, such as declaring variables or defining functions, ends up in this global
scope, and thus visible to all. Add to this the fact that JavaScript is dynamically typed, so
if two "things" were to be named the same, even if they were not the same type (variable
vs. function), there would be a collision, with the one that was evaluated last winning.

There happens to be only one construct that introduces scope, namely functions.[2]
We, the developers, quickly latched on to this idea as a mechanism to create a buffer

---

[1]https://github.com/amdjs/amdjs-api/blob/master/AMD.md
[2]We have seen how "blocks" introduce scope—however, recall that vars did not respect block
  scope, thus making it a moot point.

© Raju Gandhi 2019
R. Gandhi, *JavaScript Next*, https://doi.org/10.1007/978-1-4842-5394-6_12

between our code and the global scope, and pretty much every idea around creating modules leverages this idea.

We have discussed the idea of IEFEs in an earlier chapter, but to jog our memory here is our previous example for posterity:

```
const counter = (function createCounter() { ①
  var steps = 0; ②
  function increment() {
    steps++;
  }
  function getCount() {
    return steps;
  }

  return {
    increment,
    getCount,
  }; ③
}());

// use it
// console.log(steps); ④
counter.increment(); ⑤
console.assert(counter.getCount() === 1); ⑥
```

      ① Introduce artificial block by creating an anonymous function

      ② This `var` will be scoped within the declared function

      ③ Expose a public API by `return`-ing an object

      ④ This will result in a `ReferenceError`

      ⑤ You can use the public API

      ⑥ Invoke the public getter

IEFEs, alongside the revealing module pattern, give us exactly what we need—a mechanism to declare "private" members while allowing us to expose an API to the outside world. This is the approach most libraries in the open source ecosystem use.

However, while this seems to have solved the problem of *producing* an encapsulated construct, it does little to alleviate the problem of consuming it.

Consider jQuery as an example. jQuery wrapped all of its functionality in an IEFE, and exposed an object to global scope, namely $. In our application code, if we wish to use $, how do we go about doing it? Well, we have to ensure that the jQuery library is loaded *first*, which would introduce $ to the global scope, and then we could go about merrily using the same in our codebase.

This is to say, the order of loading libraries matter! If we were to reorder the library list, the house of cards come tumbling down.

The core issue here is that we are using the global scope to share code, making interdependencies between different pieces of the codebase *implicit*, rather than explicit. Not to mention, we can just as easily have a collision if two or more "exported" variables have the same name. This problem is further exaggerated when there are lots of mini-libraries being loaded, with interdependencies between all of them—trying to ascertain the order of loading, while avoiding collisions quickly becomes a case of Russian roulette.

Summarizing, IEFEs and the revealing module pattern can help with encapsulation, but they don't namespace what it is they are providing, leaving it to consumers to ensure that there are no collisions. On the other hand, consuming these libraries involves meticulously loading libraries in the right order, since the only shared context is the global scope.

Before we go about exploring a solution to this problem, we must consider another facet of JavaScript, that is, JavaScript is no longer just a client-side language. Developers have embraced JavaScript on the server using technologies like Node,[3] which has a completely different set of parameters as compared to client-side scripting.

Consider how JavaScript is loaded in the browser. This is done using `script` tags, which require that the browser request a resource from the server. Needless to say, we would not want to do this synchronously, since it would block the main thread, so this loading is typically done asynchronously. Contrast this with server-side programming. When one piece of the codebase "require"-s another, that script can be loaded synchronously, since it resides right there—on disk, be that in the same project, or in the `node_modules` folder.

---

[3]`https://nodejs.org/en/`

Again, the problem here is loading the libraries we need, in the right order, and making their public members available to us, without the risk of collisions. *How* these dependencies get resolved is a separate question. In the following sections we will discuss how ES6 tackles module declaration and usage. However, before we begin, let us see how we can run the code snippets in this chapter.

# How to Run Modularized JavaScript

The easiest way to run the code samples in this chapter is to use Node.[4] Node, at the time of this writing, is at version 12+, and supports ES6 modules behind an experimental flag.

First, ensure that you either have Node installed, or are running a relatively recent version of Node. Of course, if you already have a version of Node running on your machine that you want to keep around, you can use either "Node Version Manager"[5] or "nvm-windows"[6] to install and maintain multiple versions of Node simultaneously. Once installed, open a command prompt and type the following:

```
node --version
# on my machine I see 'v12.4.0'
```

If you see a valid response, then you have Node installed correctly.

In order to load and run ES6 modules in Node, there are two requirements:

- Node must be invoked with the `--experimental-modules` flag.

- Any source file that is to be treated as an ES6 module should have the file extension `.mjs` (versus being just `.js`).

Let us consider a simple example to make things clearer. `cd` to a scratch directory, and create a new file with the name `exporter.mjs` with the following contents:

```
// file name must end in "mjs" — like exporter.mjs
export const sayHello = name => `Hello ${name}!!`
```

Now create another file, in the same directory, and name it `importer.mjs` and include the following:

---

[4]https://nodejs.org/en/
[5]https://github.com/nvm-sh/nvm
[6]https://github.com/coreybutler/nvm-windows

```
import { sayHello } from './exporter.mjs'; ①
// prints 'Hello ES6 Modules!!'
console.log(sayHello("ES6 Modules"));
```

① Import members from exporter

Be sure to save both files, then in the console type the following:

```
node --experimental-modules importer.mjs
```

You should see Hello ES6 Modules!!.[7]

In our setup, `exporter.mjs` "exports" certain members, and `importer.mjs` uses said members within itself. As you play along with the examples in this chapter, you may name your files any which way, as long as the file has the `.mjs` file extension and you are using Node's experimental support for ES6 modules. The .mjs file extension is unique to Node, which by default supports CommonJS. However, ES6 module files are no different than regular JavaScript files, except that they declare a module, and hence *should* have the `.js` extension. Correspondingly, the snippets in this chapter will reference any and all files using the `.js` extension—simply replace those with `.mjs` in your workspace.

Let's talk modules!

# Declaring Modules

A module in ES6 is simply a collection of related variables, constants, functions, and classes. Modules allow us to split up our codebase into smaller, self-contained pieces of functionality, which can then be consumed by other parts of our codebase, or even published to be consumed by other applications. A module allows us to "tuck" functionality in a namespace, thereby eliminating naming conflicts.

Modules in ES6 are encompassed in files, wherein there is a one-to-one relationship between a file and a module. The name of the module is the (absolute or relative) path to the file itself. Modules operate under `strict mode` by default, which we have discussed briefly in Chapter 1. All members of a module are implicitly "private"—that is, they are

---

[7]You might see a warning about the module loader being experimental. We can ignore that for the length of this discussion.

not visible to anyone using this module unless they are explicitly export-ed. Consider the following:

```
export const degreesToRadians = d => d * (Math.PI / 180); ①
export const gradiansToRadians = g => g * 15.707 * Math.pow(10, -3);

const calc = (fn, x, unit) => { ②
  switch (unit) {
    case 'degrees':
      return fn.call(null, degreesToRadians(x));
    case 'gradians':
      return fn.call(null, gradiansToRadians(x));
    default:
      return fn.call(null, x);
  }
};

export const sin = (x, unit = 'degrees') => calc(Math.sin, x, unit);
export const cos = (x, unit = 'degrees') => calc(Math.cos, x, unit);
export const tan = (x, unit = 'degrees') => calc(Math.tan, x, unit);

export const trig = { ③
  degreesToRadians,
  gradiansToRadians,
  sin,
  cos,
  tan,
};
```

① Explicitly export-ing members

② These are private to the module

③ export an object wrapping all public members circa revealing module pattern

Here we declare a bunch of trigonometry functions, exporting those we deem our public API, and leaving the rest to be private. Note that we also export an object that holds all the public members as properties, much like we did using the revealing module pattern. This is a useful technique that gives our consumers a choice—they can pick and choose the specific functionality that they are interested in, or use the wholly exported object and have everything tucked underneath that object available to them. These exported members, also referred to as "named" exports, will be visible to anyone using this module.

export-ing individual members may prove to be verbose, and perhaps obfuscates what the public API actually is. An alternative syntax is offered that can help with this:

```
const degreesToRadians = d => d * (Math.PI / 180); ①
const gradiansToRadians = g => g * 15.707 * Math.pow(10, -3);

const calc = (fn, x, unit) => {
  switch (unit) {
    case 'degrees':
      return fn.call(null, degreesToRadians(x));
    case 'gradians':
      return fn.call(null, gradiansToRadians(x));
    default:
      return fn.call(null, x);
  }
};

const sin = (x, unit = 'degrees') => calc(Math.sin, x, unit);
const cos = (x, unit = 'degrees') => calc(Math.cos, x, unit);
const tan = (x, unit = 'degrees') => calc(Math.tan, x, unit);

const trig = {
  degreesToRadians,
  gradiansToRadians,
  sin,
  cos,
  tan,
};

export { ②
  degreesToRadians,
  gradiansToRadians,
  sin,
  cos,
  tan,
```

```
  trig,
};
```

&#9312; Define all of our members

&#9313; Use the alternative export syntax

Rather than explicitly exporting each member explicitly as we did earlier, we export all public members in one fell swoop. This can help make the public API much more explicit—however, while the public API certainly becomes obvious, maintaining the module becomes just a tad more tedious, as one must align disparate parts of the file while ascertaining what is public, and what isn't.

Whether we export each member explicitly or export in one fell swoop is a matter of taste and preference. However, it seems that the JavaScript community as a whole seems to be tipping toward explicitly exporting each public member. Furthermore, documentation tools like ESDoc[8] intelligently only reveal exported members, thereby making the public API obvious even with explicit exporting.

We can also export a "default" member, which is a means to express the "one single" thing that module exports. Consider a situation where we are writing a math library, and we happen to have a trigonometry module, wherein we are simply defining all of our trigonometry functions. Given that this is all there is to this module, a default export makes sense.

However, this can be confusing, because we are allowed to mix and match having a default member, while explicitly exporting other members, like so:

```
export {  &#9312;
  degreesToRadians,
  gradiansToRadians,
  sin,
  cos,
  tan,  &#9313;
};

export default trig;  &#9314;
```

&#9312; Explicitly export our public members

---

[8]https://esdoc.org/

② Note that we are no longer exporting `trig`

③ Make `trig` a default export for this module

Here, we use the `default` keyword to export our all-inclusive `trig` object, which we assume is what most of our clients will want to use anyway. However, we can still export individual members in case our clients rather order à la carte instead of a full entrée. (One can also use the inline named export mechanism, or use both in combination if one so desires.) Needless to say, as the name suggests, there can only be one default export.

While default exports seem like a good idea, default exports are a transitionary mechanism since this is the model that CommonJs[9] uses, and come with more than their share of downsides.

Unlike named exports (as the name suggests), default exports do not expose the name of the exported member to the outside world. This shifts the onus to the consumers of that module, who then decide what to call that export. Consider `degreesToRadians` which happens to be a named export—the world sees and uses this member with the same name. If we were to change `degreesToRadians` to `degToRad`, then anyone using this module will be forced to make the same change. However, `trig`, being a default export, does not force a consumer to call it `trig`. This means that if we were to rename trig, the client would not see that change, thus making refactoring efforts rather tedious. Having no name also means that editors that support IntelliSense cannot help with auto-completion of symbols or auto-importing. Finally, default exports limit the ability for build tools to do any form of tree-shaking a.k.a dead code elimination.[10]

Furthermore, using named exports can help anyone using our modules (which may include us) make our production bundle size smaller, aid development practices like refactoring, and, as we will see soon, reduce confusion when importing the module. All this to say, using default exports is largely considered an anti-pattern[11] and we should use this feature at a minimum, if at all.

There is one more facility that exports provide us, which is aliasing. Let us take a look to see how this works for named exports.

---

[9]https://requirejs.org/docs/commonjs.html

[10]https://medium.com/@rauschma/note-that-default-exporting-objects-is-usually-an-anti-pattern-if-you-want-to-export-the-cf674423ac38

[11]https://humanwhocodes.com/blog/2019/01/stop-using-default-exports-javascript-module/

# Aliasing Exports

Aliasing exports allows us to rename members of the module, so that the name that we reference a member with internally to the module is different from the name that consumers see it as. This might prove to be valuable if one wishes to completely decouple the module from its consumers, leaving us free to refactor names without affecting the outside world. The syntax, as expressed here, is rather unsurprising:

```
// code abbreviated for brevity
export {
  degreesToRadians,
  gradiansToRadians,
  sin as sine, ①
  cos as cosine,
  tan,
  trig as trignometry, ②
};
```

① Explicitly export our public members

② Export our all-encompassing object as well with an alias

The as syntax works as advertised, allowing us to rename our member **on the way out**. Now, we are free to rename any of our aliased members internally any which way we want, without forcing all of our consumers to refactor as well.

Aliasing exports reveals another shortcoming of default exports, namely since default exports are unnamed exports, aliasing them is a meaningless proposition.

# A Quick Summary

Summarizing, exporting implies making members of a module public, that is, they are accessible to consumers of the module. We have seen two separate mechanisms for exporting—named export, which can be inlined, and therefore individual exports, vs. exporting all symbols in one fell swoop. Alternatively, we also saw the syntax for default exports, and discussed some of the cons of using this approach.

Let us now turn toward the other side of the equation, namely importing or consuming a module.

# Importing

ES6 introduces the `import` keyword that allows one module to import another. Only modules can use other modules—modules **cannot** be consumed from plain old JavaScript files. Also, recall that modules and files have a one-to-one relationship, in that, a file contains one and only one module, and the name of the contained module is the name of the file itself.

The `import` syntax consists of two parts—the name of the module and what to import from the said module. Specifying which module is simply specifying the path to the location of the module. The interesting bit here are the mechanisms to actually import exported members, so let us talk about that.

How one imports members of another module depends on how those members were exported to begin with. As we know, a module can export named and default members. We begin with how we can work with named members.

Consuming a module that has named exports forces the consumer to use the same name as the exported members. Consider the following:

```
/*
'030-named-exports' exports the following
export {
  degreesToRadians,
  gradiansToRadians,
  sin,
  cos,
  tan,
  trig,
}
*/
import { ①
  sin,
  cos,
```

```
  tan,
} from './030-named-exports';

// use the functions
console.log(sin(0));
```

① Import the members required for this module

A few points of note regarding **how** we import the pieces we are interested in from another module. The import syntax looks very similar to the destructuring syntax we saw in a previous chapter. We are also allowed to pick and choose the members we are interested in, thus permitting the import of only certain members although the module might export a lot more.

Recall that the name of the member is **whatever** was exported from the module. So, if the members being exported are aliased, then we must import the aliased names:

```
/*
'050-alias-exports' exports the following
export {
  degreesToRadians,
  gradiansToRadians,
  sin as sine,
  cos as cosine,
  tan,
  trig as trignometry,
};
*/

import {
  sine, ①
  cosine,
  tan,
  trignometry,
} from './050-alias-exports';
```

① Use the aliased names in the import

The module we rely on aliases its members; therefore, as far as any consuming module is concerned, those are the public names, and therefore the only ones available for import.

What if we wanted to import all exported members of another module? The import syntax supports the wildcard (*) syntax with one caveat—the import must then be namespaced as shown here:

*Importing named members*

```
/*
'050-alias-exports' exports the following
export {
  degreesToRadians,
  gradiansToRadians,
  sin as sine,
  cos as cosine,
  tan,
  trig as trignometry,
};
*/
import * as trigFns from './050-alias-exports'; ①

console.log(trigFns.sine(0)); ②
```

① Use the wildcard operator to import all the exported members in one fell swoop

② Tucked under the namespace members are visible using their public name

Using the wildcard operator increases the changes of collisions between names, especially if a large number of other modules are being imported. The `as` namespacing attempts to eliminate this possibility. Correspondingly, if we import two separate modules accidentally with the same name, we will get an error.

# Aliasing Imports

There is a chance that one or more modules being imported may export members with the same name; in which case, we need a mechanism to resolve name collisions. This is not an issue when we use the wildcard syntax since the imports are namespaced to begin with. However, if we are importing individual members of a module, and we have to resolve conflicts, we can alias an import just like we can alias exports:

```
/*
'030-named-exports' exports the following
export {
  degreesToRadians,
  gradiansToRadians,
  sin,
  cos,
  tan,
  trig,
}
*/

import {
  sin as sine, ①
  cos as cosine,
  trig as trignometry,
} from './030-named-exports';
```

① Alias imports

Aliasing imports, outside of aiding in avoiding collisions, also allows us to "rename" functions that perhaps might be too long, or help them fit better with the domain we are working with.

Default exports, once again, prove to be a problem child. Since default exports are unnamed exports, the consuming module can call that default export anything they want!

```
/*
'040-default-exports' exports the following
export {
```

```
  degreesToRadians,
  gradiansToRadians,
  sin,
  cos,
  tan,
};

export default trig;
*/
import myTrignometry, { ①
  sin,
  cos,
  tan,
} from './040-default-exports';

console.log(myTrignometry.sin()); ②
```

① Import the default giving it an arbitrary name

② Use the default import just as we would any other member

Often times, when modules export default members, since the name of the import is not mandated, different consumers within the same project refer to the default export using different names, making it incredibly hard to find where a member is being used. This forces developers working with such exports to settle on a naming convention in an attempt to bring the naming to parity with named exports.[12]

The syntax for importing, much like exporting, is rather flexible, and we can mix and match any and all combinations of imports. We could, for example, import the default, along with other named members with aliasing if we wish to do so:

```
/*
'040-default-exports' exports the following
export {
  degreesToRadians,
  gradiansToRadians,
```

---

[12]For example, react.js exports a default (https://github.com/facebook/react/blob/659a29c ecf74301532354261369e9048aac6e20f/packages/react/src/React.js#L71) and developers idiomatically import it as React. However, there is no language construct to enforce it.

```
  sin,
  cos,
  tan,
};

export default trig;
*/
import myTrignometry, { ①
  sin as sine, ②
  cos as cosine,
  tan,
} from './040-default-exports';

console.log(myTrignometry.sin()); ③
console.log(sine(45));
```

① Import the default with any name

② Import named members with aliases

③ Use the imports just like we would any other time

The primary driving force behind the import style remains on how a module exports its members. Simultaneously, features like aliasing imports in a particular module *may* be driven by considerations like avoiding name collisions, or attempting to make the imported functions seem more accommodating to the domain at hand. However, we must persevere to refrain from using these features from a stylistic mindset, so as to not introduce too much overhead on anyone who is attempting to maintain the codebase.

# Caveats and Implications

The syntax for ES6 modules is designed around exports and imports being "static"— in that, they need to be top-level statements in module files. We are **not** allowed to dynamically or conditionally export or import members.[13]

There are several benefits to having static modules, with faster lookup, smaller bundles (if we are to use a bundling tool like Webpack or Rollup) due to deterministic

---

[13]There is a proposal (`https://github.com/tc39/proposal-dynamic-import`) that allows for dynamic imports; however, at the time this chapter was written, it remains a Stage 3.

dead code elimination. You can read more about the benefits of this approach in this exemplary blog post (`http://calculist.org/blog/2012/06/29/static-module-resolution/`) by Dave Herman.

# Summary

Phew! Who thought that packaging our code to be easily consumable would be this tricky? While it may seem that the module syntax introduced in ES6 is overkill, we must bear in mind that JavaScript is a language that straddles both sides of the wire, in that, it runs in the browser and on the server. Therefore, it will serve us well to remember that any syntax added for modules needs to accommodate both ecosystems.

In the next chapter, we will explore proxies that allow us to magically adorn both new and existing objects with additional functionality without actually modifying the objects themselves.

.

CHAPTER 13

# Metamorphosis with Proxy and Reflect

No API can or should attempt to be complete. Depending on the use-case, and the problem space, we often find that we may need to add, remove, or even constraint behavior to an object, or a type. Historically our approach to this was leveraging JavaScript's dynamic nature, and simply tack on the additional behavior we wanted to see on any object. Symbols can help in this regard, by giving us the guarantee of collision-free keys. However, in many cases it can feel a tad hackish, especially when we do not wish to *permanently* modify behavior of an object for the lifetime of our application.

ES6 gives us proxies, which are essentially an implementation of the proxy pattern at a language level. In this chapter we will see how we can change the behavior of both new and existing objects without actually modifying the objects themselves, while simultaneously giving us the ability to explicitly opt-in and opt-out if and when we choose to do so.

## The Perils of Monkey-patching

JavaScript is a dynamically typed language, in that, it does not require us to know or declare what the type of a variable or object is upfront. This dynamic nature can be extended to the structure of objects, wherein, given an object, we can modify its properties (and methods) to suit our needs. This flexibility of JavaScript, along with other features intrinsic to the language like prototypal inheritance and first-class functions, has proven to be one of the selling points of JavaScript, allowing developers to drum up

© Raju Gandhi 2019
R. Gandhi, *JavaScript Next*, https://doi.org/10.1007/978-1-4842-5394-6_13

powerful yet elegant solutions like aspect-oriented programming facilities[1] and Behavior Driven Testing using mocks and spies with Sinon,[2] at the risk of it being abused.[3]

One particular set of (ab)use-cases lies with adding behavior to existing types and objects. Consider a scenario where anytime we get or set a property on an object, we wish to automatically perform a side effect, like logging. This isn't something we would want done everywhere, since it might prove to be verbose, expensive, or both. We could, using JavaScript's dynamic nature, modify the behavior for a certain section of the codebase, carefully reverting it back to its original behavior afterward, like so:

```
const intercept = (obj, interceptionFn) => { ①
  for (const m in obj) {
    if ((Object.prototype.hasOwnProperty.call(obj, m)) && (obj[m]
    instanceof Function)) { ②
      const method = obj[m]; ③
      obj[m] = function(...args) {
        interceptionFn.call(obj, m); ④
        return method.apply(obj, args); ⑤
      };
    }
  }
};

const logger = m => console.log(`${m} was called`); ⑥
const toBeIntercepted = { ⑦
  name: 'Jonathan',
  getName() {
    return this.name;
  },
  setName(name) {
    this.name = name;
  },
};
```

---

[1]https://github.com/k1r0s/kaop
[2]https://sinonjs.org/
[3]Anyone remember eval??

```
intercept(toBeIntercepted, logger); ⑧
```

```
// prints 'getName was called' followed by 'Jonathan'
console.log(toBeIntercepted.getName());
// prints 'setName was called'
toBeIntercepted.setName('Johnson');
// prints 'getName was called' followed by 'Johnson'
console.log(toBeIntercepted.getName());
```

① Define our interceptor function

② Ensure that we only intercept the supplied objects methods

③ Grab a reference to the method

④ Call the interception function first

⑤ Then delegate to the original method

⑥ Define our "logger" function

⑦ Define a plain JavaScript object

⑧ Be sure to modify the object prior to invoking its methods

We start with writing a rather generic method-intercepting function that takes two arguments—the object whose behavior we wish to modify and the function that is to be invoked when any of the object's method gets called. Then we loop over all of the supplied objects properties, ensuring that we do **not** climb the inheritance tree, and only modifying properties that happen to be methods. Finally, we define our "logger" function and an object, and ensure we decorate the methods of the object so that our logger function is called upon every invocation.

In this case we are modifying the behavior of an existing object for certain pieces of functionality, namely any method invocation. That said, our implementation makes it hard to turn off the newly introduced behavior. In order to revert the behavior to its original behavior, we will have to store the original implementations of the methods we modify, and then reinstall them.

Of course, we risk forgetting to turn off the behavior (assuming that we can), and suffer the consequences, including leaking unintended behavior elsewhere, and surprising any other unwitting clients with unexpected side effects. This technique of modifying existing behavior is used very effectively by testing libraries like Sinon to create spies and mocks, and present an ideal use-case—testing limits the scope in which the new behavior is visible.

This argument can be extended to objects that we did not create, and therefore do not own. Consider the use of an array. What if we wanted to make it so arrays could be compared? They would compare their individual items, recursing if the item itself happens to be a nested array. Here is one approach:

```
Object.defineProperty(Array.prototype, 'equals', { ①
  value(other) {
    if (!other) return false;
    if (!Array.isArray(other)) return false;
    if (this.length !== other.length) return false;

    const [fMe, ...rMe] = this;
    const [fOther, ...rOther] = other;

    if (fMe === fOther) {
      return true;
    }

    if ((rMe.length === 0) && (rOther.length === 0)) {
      return true;
    }
    return rMe.equals(rOther);
  },
  enumerable: false,
  configurable: true,
});

const first = [1, 2, 3, [4, 5]];
const second = [1, 2, 3, [4, 5]];
const third = [1, 2, 3];

// prints 'true'
console.log(first.equals(second)); ②
// prints 'false'
console.log(first.equals(third));
```

① Use Object.defineProperty to add an equals method

② Voila! Now that method is available on every array

In this example we use `Object.defineProperty` to define an `equals` method on `Arrays` prototype. We could just as easily tacked the property using `Array.prototype.equals = function() { … }`; however, using `Object.defineProperty` gives us a chance to configure the visibility of this new method—setting `enumerable` to `false` hides the property from `for-in` loops. At the same time, we set its `configurable` property to `true`, thus allowing us to delete the property if we choose to do so.

Note that in this case we are augmenting `Arrays`, rather than modifying the behavior of existing methods on an array.

In languages like Ruby and Python, any modification of an existing type or object at runtime is referred to as "monkey patching."[4] This can be very useful—for example Ruby on Rails[5] uses this technique to great benefit; however, if not executed or documented properly, it can prove to be very confusing or even pernicious.

In addition to modification and augmentation of behavior, there are other enhancements or restrictions we might want to affect—returning reasonable defaults for undefined properties, tacking on methods dynamically, constraining construction of objects so we are using a singleton, the list goes on. Ideally, we should be able to modify behavior in a manner that is unobtrusive, **and** namespaced, or isolated to specific parts of our application, wherein we intentionally ask for the modified behavior, knowing that we have in no way affected the behavior of the original object. In response, ES6 introduces `Proxy`, alongside `Reflect`. While the two offer a slew of functionality on their own, together they make a remarkable tag team.

# Metaprogramming with Proxy and Reflect

ES6 `Proxy` class, as the name suggests, allows us to implement the Proxy pattern[6] as a language-level construct. It allows us to create a proxy that wraps the object we wish to enhance or modify. However, since it has language level support, we can intercept or proxy basic operations like getting/setting/adding/deleting properties and constructor calls for objects and invocations for functions. In other words, `Proxy` lets us hook into the internal machinery of JavaScript itself.

---

[4]`https://en.wikipedia.org/wiki/Monkey_patch`
[5]`https://rubyonrails.org/`
[6]`https://en.wikipedia.org/wiki/Proxy_pattern`

The mechanism to intercede and thereby modify behavior is through the use of a "handler" object that has "traps" defined. If we do not define a trap for a particular piece of functionality, the proxy rightly forwards the call to the original object.

Let us start with a simple example of a proxy and a handler, and we will then delve into all of the moving parts that make proxies awesome in ES6.

```
const toBeIntercepted = { ①
  name: 'Jonathan',
  getName() {
    return this.name;
  },
  setName(name) {
    this.name = name;
  },
};

const proxied = new Proxy(toBeIntercepted, ②
  { ③
    get(target, property) { ④
      console.log(`${property} was called`);
      return target[property];
    },
  },
);

// prints 'name was called', followed by 'Jonathan'
console.log(proxied.name); ⑤
// prints 'getName was called', followed by 'Jonathan'
console.log(proxied.getName());
```

① An object we wish to augment

② Construct a proxy

③ Provide the proxy with a handler

④ Define the "get" trap

⑤ Use the proxy

We construct a proxy *around* an object using the `Proxy` constructor, which takes two arguments—the object we wish to proxy and a handler object that has traps defined on it. The traps are functions with very specific[7] names and signatures, each one targeting a specific piece of JavaScript's internal mechanisms. The proxy invokes the appropriate trap, passing it a reference to the original object, the name of the property that was looked up, as well as a reference to the proxy object.

Note that the proxy makes no attempt to modify the original object! Instead it hands us a *new* object, that has been adorned with the new behavior—however, we may still hold a reference to the original object, reverting back to it if we so desire.

Our initial attempt might be rather simplistic, but we can see the beginnings of how we can use proxies to accomplish some rather mind-altering metaprogramming magic in JavaScript. Let us extend our proxy implementation to recreate intercepting all method calls on an object:

```
const intercept = (obj, interceptionFn) => { ①
  const handler = { ②
    get(target, property) {
      if ((Reflect.has(target, property))
        && (target[property] instanceof Function)) { ③
        interceptionFn.call(target, property); ④
      }
      return Reflect.get(target, property); ⑤
    },
  };
  return new Proxy(obj, handler); ⑥
};

const logger = m => console.log(`${m} was called`); ⑦
const toBeIntercepted = { ⑧
  name: 'Jonathan',
  getName() {
    return this.name;
  },
  setName(name) {
```

---

[7]https://developer.mozilla.org/en-US/docs/Web/JavaScript/Reference/Global_Objects/ Proxy/handler

```
    this.name = name;
  },
};
const proxied = intercept(toBeIntercepted, logger); ⑨

// prints 'getName was called' followed by 'Jonathan'
console.log(proxied.getName());
// prints 'setName was called'
proxied.setName('Johnson');
// prints 'getName was called' followed by 'Johnson'
console.log(proxied.getName());
```

① Define a wrapper function to create a proxy

② Our handler with the get trap

③ Ensure that we only intercept the supplied objects methods

④ Call the interception function first

⑤ Then delegate to the original method

⑥ Return the proxy

⑦ Define our "logger" function

⑧ Define a plain JavaScript object

⑨ Be sure to wrap our object with the proxy and use that going forward

Our attempt does not depart from our earlier attempt at intercepting method calls on objects with the exception of using proxies. However, we gain a lot of benefits—we no longer mutate the object; instead, the proxy allows us to accomplish exactly what we want, allowing us to revert back to the original behavior by simply switching references. Since the proxy itself is a reference, it can be scoped in a function or a module. Leaving this scope translates to the world never knowing that the proxy even exists!

We did subtly introduce using the Reflect API here, so you might be wondering—what's all that about? Reflect is a new API that landed alongside Proxy in ES6, and serves as a mirror API to the handler for proxies. Thus, for every kind of trap we are able to install on a proxy's handler, there exists a static property on `Reflect`.[8] Anytime we define a trap on a handler, and we wish to forward the same call to the original object, we can simply use the mirrored `Reflect` API, passing in the target object and any arguments that it may need. In our example we are trapping get—however, after calling our interception function, we wish to forward the call to the original object, so we can just use `Reflect.get`.

We have had a taste of how to use proxies, and the `Reflect` API. Now we will attempt to recreate our earlier example of defining an `equals` method without monkey-patching `Array.prototype` itself. Recall that in this case, we are attempting to augment arrays with a new method, namely `equals`. We will start by writing a recursive function that can compare one array (referenced by `this`) with another array:

```
const equals = function (other) {
  if (!other) return false;
  if (!Array.isArray(other)) return false;
  if (this.length !== other.length) return false;

  const [fMe, ...rMe] = this;
  const [fOther, ...rOther] = other;

  if (fMe === fOther) {
    return true;
  }
  if ((rMe.length === 0) && (rOther.length === 0)) {
    return true;
  }
  return rMe.equals(rOther);
};
```

Next, we will write our handler, which will intercept any calls to `equals` and dispatches the call to our newly minted `equals` method:

```
const comparableArray = (arr) => { ①
  const handler = { ②
```

---

[8]You can see this for yourself simply by using `for(const m of Reflect.ownKeys(Reflect)) { console.log(m); }` and comparing the list with the list found at `https://developer.mozilla.org/en-US/docs/Web/JavaScript/Reference/Global_Objects/Proxy/handler`.

```
    get(target, property) { ③
      if (property === 'equals') { ④
        return equals;
      }
      return Reflect.get(target, property); ⑤
    },
  };
  return new Proxy(arr, handler);
};

const first = comparableArray([1, 2, 3, [4, 5]]);
const second = comparableArray([1, 2, 3, [4, 5]]);
const third = comparableArray([1, 2, 3]);

// prints 'true'
console.log(first.equals([1, 2, 3, [4, 5]])); ②
// prints 'false'
console.log(first.equals(third));
```

      ① Define our proxy creator helper

      ② Define our handler

      ③ Trap get

      ④ Augment any calls for the equal method

      ⑤ Otherwise delegate to the original object

We once again trap a get, except this time, if the property that is being sought out happens to be equals, we return our custom implementation; otherwise, simply forward the call to the original object. Although our equals implementation does not in any way differ from our earlier attempt, our approach is significantly different. We gain new behavior via the proxy, without having to monkey-patch Array itself.

This augmentation is visible to only those who use the proxy. Furthermore, since the proxy delegates to the original object for anything outside of get-ing the equals method, for any other consumer of the proxy, the modification is completely transparent.

# Enforcing Singletons

Perhaps now we can see how we can accomplish a many a nifty feature like adding methods or modifying existing methods. Let us consider another use-case wherein we use proxies to build the singleton pattern.[9] In order to achieve this, we will have to trap the construction of an object, ensuring that once we have an instance, we always return that instance. A glance at the MDN documentation leads us to `handler.construct`[10]– perfect! Just what we need.

```
const singletonFactory = (constructorFn) => { ①
  let instance; ②
  const handler = {
    construct(target, args) { ③
      if (!instance) {
        instance = Reflect.construct(constructorFn, args); ④
      }
      return instance; ⑤
    },
  };
  return new Proxy(constructorFn, handler);
};

class SuperHeroService { ⑥
  constructor() {
    this.heroes = [
      'IronMan',
      'Captain America',
      'Wasp',
      'Black Widow',
    ];
  }

  getHeroes() {
```

[9]https://en.wikipedia.org/wiki/Singleton_pattern
[10]https://developer.mozilla.org/en-US/docs/Web/JavaScript/Reference/Global_Objects/ Proxy/handler/construct

```
    return this.heroes;
  }

  addHero(hero) {
    this.heroes.push(hero);
  }
}

const SingletonSuperHeroService = singletonFactory(SuperHeroService); ⑦

const service1 = new SingletonSuperHeroService();
const service2 = new SingletonSuperHeroService(); ⑧
// prints 'true'
console.log(service1 === service2); ⑨
```

① Define our proxy helper

② A local variable to cache our instance

③ Trap the constructor call

④ If we do not have an instance, invoke the supplied constructor

⑤ Otherwise we return our cached instance

⑥ A class we wish to treat as a singleton

⑦ Create the proxy

⑧ Multiple calls to the proxy return the same instance

⑨ Ensure that the instances are the same

Our proxy creator function expects to get the constructor of the object we wish to make a singleton as its sole argument. Our implementation, save for trapping the construct, is rather unimpressive—we hold a local reference to the singleton if and when we create it, and upon subsequent invocation of the constructor simply return the same reference. As we can see, we can wrap any constructor that we wish to treat as a singleton with this simple implementation. Multiple invocations of the proxied constructor simply return the same instance.

# Building a DSL

Finally, let us see what it takes to build a simple domain-specific language (DSL) using proxies. We will attempt to tackle a rather popular domain, namely that of building XML markup. However, we will have to take a shortcut; our DSL will only produce the necessary JSON that can be consumed by a tool like FreeFormatter.com's "JSON to XML Converter."[11] This will allow us to keep our focus on leveraging proxies for such scenarios.

This tool (by default) assumes that all attributes for elements are prefixed by a @, and the element's text be prefixed by #. Thus, given the following snippet of JSON:

```
{
  "books": {
    "@count": "1",
    "book": {
      "@id": "1",
      "title": {
        "@isbn": "1590592395",
        "#text": "Practical Common Lisp"
      }
    }
  }
}
```

The tool will produce the equivalent XML:

```
<?xml version="1.0" encoding="UTF-8"?>
<root>
  <books count="1">
    <book id="1">
      <title isbn="1590592395">Practical Common Lisp</title>
    </book>
  </books>
</root>
```

---

[11]www.freeformatter.com/json-to-xml-converter.html

This is what our DSL[12] will look like:

```
const books = jsonToXmlBuilder()
                .books({ count: '1' })
                  .book({ id: '1' })
                    .title({ isbn: '1590592395' }, 'Practical Common Lisp')
                    .up()
                  .up()
                .end();
console.log(books);
// prints
// {
//    "books": {
//      "@count": "1",
//        "book": {
//        "@id": "1",
//          "title": {
//          "@isbn": "1590592395",
//          "#text": "Practical Common Lisp"
//        }
//      }
//    }
// }
```

Our DSL has a few characteristics:

Elements are expressed as methods, and can be nested.

Elements can be supplied with an object that represents its attributes, and the text of the element.

The up method takes us back up to the parent Node so we can add additional child elements to the same parent if we desire to do so.

The end method signals the end of the chain, and produces the requisite JSON.

---

[12]Our DSL is heavily influenced by https://github.com/oozcitak/xmlbuilder-js/wiki.

Excited? Let's get started! First, we will write a one-argument helper function to build an element. This function, in turn returns a function, that expects to be supplied the attributes and text for an element, and simply constructs the necessary JSON to represent that element. This function `returns` the proxy object itself, which will be in scope once we are done with our implementation. Here is what our ele-ment builder looks like:

```
const ele = function(target) { ①
  return function (attrs = {}, text = '') {
    for(const [k, v] of Object.entries(attrs)) {
      target[`@${k}`] = v; ②
    }
    if(text) target['#text'] = text; ③
    // this will be in scope
    return proxy;
  }
}
```

       ① Our function takes a target object

      ② We loop over all attributes supplied, and tack it on the target

      ③ If the text is supplied, tack that on as well

Our ele function is rather simple—it accepts a `target` object, then constructs a two-argument function that is eventually returned. This newly constructed function expects two (optional) arguments—an object representing the attributes for this element and the text. We loop over the `entries` in the attributes object, tacking on each one on the target with the prerequisite @ prefix. If any text is supplied, that too is tacked on to the target prefixed with #.

*Assuming* we have something called proxy in scope, we can use this function like so:

```
const obj = {};
const builder = ele(obj); ①
builder({ isbn: '1590592395' }, 'Practical Common Lisp'); ②
// prints '{ '@isbn': '1590592395', '#text': 'Practical Common Lisp' }'
console.log(obj);
```

① Returns the inner function

② Invoke the returned function with some attributes, and some text

As we can see here, attributes are to be supplied as an object, wherein each key-value entry represents an attribute. This allows us to supply multiple attributes. The `ele` function simply constructs a function (referenced by `builder`); this function in turn, when invoked with attributes and some text, attaches the necessary metadata onto the `target`.

Great! Now, we will write our proxy handler function.

```
// 'elements' is a stack of previously constructed elements,
// initialized with an empty object (the root)
// Every time we encounter a new element, we put it at the
// top of the stack.
// Every time we encounter an 'up()', we drop the top-most entry
const handler = {
  get(target, property) {
    if (property === 'end') {
      return () => JSON.stringify(elements.pop()); ①
    }
    if (property === 'up') {
      elements.shift(); ②
      return () => proxy; ③
    }
    const [curParent] = elements; ④
    const child = {};
    elements.unshift(child); ⑤
    if(curParent[property]) { ⑥
      const existing = curParent[property];
      if(Array.isArray(existing)) {
        curParent[property] = [...existing, child];
      } else {
        curParent[property] = [existing, child];
      }
    } else {
```

```
      curParent[property] = child;
    }
    return ele(child); ⑦
  },
};
```

① If we are at the end, simply `stringify` the last element in the stack

② If we are going up, then drop the top-most element

③ Since up is a method, upon invocation return the `proxy` itself

④ Get the top-most element in the stack

⑤ Push the latest element on top of the stack

⑥ Cater for an element we have already seen

⑦ Return the mechanism to adorn the latest element with attributes and text

There is a lot going on here, so let us take it one step at a time. XML allows for nesting, permitting an element to have any number of children. In order to track the "current" element (without losing track of all of its parents) we maintain a stack, namely `elements`, that happens to be an array of previously constructed elements. That is, the "root" element will always be the *last* element in the array.

When we encounter an `end()` we simply `JSON.stringify` the last element in the array by invoking pop. Note that invoking `end` results in the JSON string being returned, thereby signaling the end of our DSL chain.

Whenever the client invokes `up()` we simply drop the *first* element in the stack, thereby making its "parent" the element that will be affected by the next operation. Here we must be careful to return the `proxy` to allow for a fluent API; this allows for the chaining to continue.

Finally, we get to the meat of our implementation. We get the first element in the `elements` array using the destructuring syntax.[13] We construct a placeholder for the child element (an empty object) and insert it at the top of the `elements` stack, thus making it the "current" element.

---

[13]The `elements` array will be initialized with an empty object as its first entry.

Next, we associate the child element to the parent using the `property` as its key. However, XML allows a parent to have multiple child elements with the same name. If that were to happen, we ensure that we wrap *all* of the children with the same name in an array prior to associating it with the parent.

So now that the parent is associated with an empty child (or an array of children) with the `property` as its key, we simply return the mechanism to adorn the child with attributes and text if the user chooses to do so.

Final step, we wrap everything neatly in the `jsonToXmlBuilder` function. Note that the wrapper function includes the definitions for `ele` and `handler`:

```
const jsonToXmlBuilder = () => {
  // truncated for brevity
  // const ele = function(target) { get(target, property) { ... } }
  // const handler = { ... }
  const root = {};
  const elements = [root];
  const proxy = new Proxy(root, handler);
  return proxy;
};
```

We start with an empty `root` element, and place it as the first element in the `elements` stack. Next, we construct the `proxy` object by invoking the `Proxy` constructor, supplying it the `root` object, and the `handler` function, and return the proxy. We are done! Let's give it a spin and see how we did:

```
const books = jsonToXmlBuilder()
                .books({ count: '2' })
                  .book({ id: '1' })
                    .title({ isbn: '1590592395' }, 'Practical Common Lisp')
                    .up()
                  .up()
                  .book({ id: '2' })
                    .title({ isbn: '9780133708752' }, 'ANSI Common LISP')
                    .up()
                  .up()
                  .subject({}, "Lisp")
                  .up()
```

```
           .end();
console.log(books);
// prints
// {
//   "books": {
//     "@count": "2",
//     "book": [{
//       "@id": "1",
//       "title": {
//         "@isbn": "1590592395",
//         "#text": "Practical Common Lisp"
//       }
//     }, {
//       "@id": "2",
//       "title": {
//         "@isbn": "9780133708752",
//         "#text": "ANSI Common LISP"
//       }
//     }],
//     "subject": {
//       "#text": "Lisp"
//     }
//   }
// }
// paste the output in https://www.freeformatter.com/json-to-xml-converter.
html
// and you can verify the generated XML
```

We have unlocked "Mastery" level with proxies. This example demonstrates the true power of proxies—in about 50 lines of code, we implemented a powerful DSL that allows us to express our intent in a succinct, yet declarative manner.

# Summary

Proxy, along with Reflect, proves us with all of the tools we need to create "meta" magic in our code unobtrusively. Proxies give us namespaced wrappers around the objects we wish to enhance, ensuring that the modified behavior is only visible to the region of code where it is applicable. Reflect mirrors the API of Proxy, while simultaneously giving JavaScript a specific place to house reflection-specific APIs, whereas prior to ES6, it was Object that demonstrated some reflection capabilities. Having Reflect as part of the toolkit going forward allows JavaScript to reduce the clutter in Object, perhaps even to the point where JavaScript can begin to deprecate the usage of certain methods like getPrototypeOf and isExtensible. Both these classes allow us to approach metaprogramming in JavaScript in an elegant fashion, and I am certain that creative developers will find extremely interesting use-cases to apply these to.

Symbols allow us to sprinkle behavior onto our objects, while proxies (and reflect) allow us to modify behavior *around* our objects. Between symbols and proxies, the duality of metaprogramming is now complete. We can and should pick the right apparatus that best serves our use-case.

In the next chapter we will look at a powerful feature introduced in ES8, namely async and await, that magically allow us to treat asynchronous code like synchronous code, thereby eliminating much of the syntactical overhead when using promises.

# CHAPTER 14

# Seemingly Imperative with async and await

When working with asynchronous operations, promises present a huge leap forward from using callbacks. However, promises present us with a specific domain-specific language (DSL) to work with, including but not limited to then, catch, and finally. This DSL, while easy, and fluent to work with, does not compose well with how we typically write code in JavaScript, which is imperative code. Consider the case of trapping errors—JavaScript affords us language constructs like try/catch that allow us to trap errors, and provide meaningful stack traces. Promises on the other hand, trap errors using the catch and finally API. This departure from our traditional model of writing code introduces a mental burden as we switch between different parts of our codebase.

In this chapter we will see how async and await can help us refactor all of our codes so that we can begin to work with asynchronous code just like we do with synchronous code. We will be able to express our intent more clearly, without getting lost in a maze of callbacks, and deal with state management and error handling using concepts that we are familiar with. We will be wiping tears of joy from our faces as we come to the end of this chapter, rejoicing in how beautiful, simple, and most importantly, consistent our code seems to be.

## The Shortcomings of the Promise DSL

In JavaScript, programming asynchronously is our only weapon of choice when attempting to accomplish any long-running tasks. Promises, now a native API in ES6, attempt to tame the complexity that callbacks yield by making state management and error propagation easier. Promises are inherently wrappers around callbacks, and while they do make the code easier to reason about, they come with their own set of compromises.

© Raju Gandhi 2019
R. Gandhi, *JavaScript Next*, https://doi.org/10.1007/978-1-4842-5394-6_14

However, it turns out that code in JavaScript that works imperatively (or blocking code) and code that works asynchronously are distinctly different. Consider the following snippet where we attempt to perform a rather simple operation imperatively:

```
const firstSyncOp = () => 10; ①
const secondSyncOp = arg => arg + 20;
const thirdSyncOp = arg => arg + 30;

const firstSyncOpResult = firstSyncOp(); ②
const secondSyncOpResult = secondSyncOp(firstSyncOpResult);
const result = thirdSyncOp(secondSyncOpResult);

// prints 'Using synchronous operations 60'
console.log('Using synchronous operations', result);
```

       ① Imperative functions

      ② Do some simple operations with the results

While this example may seem a tad contrived, it serves our use-case well. We start with a couple of synchronous or blocking functions, and then proceed to do some operation, in this case simple arithmetic with the individual results.

This example, outside of being verbose, is rather simple to comprehend—we can treat the result of our individual function much like we treat any other value, waiting to use them and then calculate the final result.

Next, we will convert our blocking operations into nonblocking or asynchronous operations using promises, and attempt to achieve the same result.

```
const firstAsyncOp = () => new Promise(res => setTimeout(res, 10, 10)); ①
const secondAsyncOp = arg => new Promise(res => setTimeout(res, 10, arg + 20));
const thirdAsyncOp = arg => Promise.resolve(arg + 30);

const result = firstAsyncOp()
  .then(secondAsyncOp) ②
  .then(thirdAsyncOp);
```

```
result.then((r) => {
  console.log('Using promises', r);
  return r;
});
```

① A series of asynchronous operations

② A promise chain

This time, we pretend our operands are being fetched asynchronously—the first two after a delay of a tenth of a second, while the third being resolved immediately. However, since each operand is wrapped in a promise, we must then use the then API to chain the operations, eventually ending up with the same result as in our previous example.

If we were to compare our two attempts, although the end result is the same, the two approaches seem very different. While promises reduce the ceremony and verbosity often involved with callbacks, they do little to bring parity to how we usually work with synchronous operations. The two look nothing like one another! And this is just the tip of the iceberg.

We are used to capturing the results of intermediate operations in variables, which in turn can be used in conditionals, or looping constructs like a for loop. Consider the following example where we contrast using conditionals in imperative code vs. a promise chain:

```
let syncConditionalResult = firstSyncOp();
if (syncConditionalResult > 20) { ①
  syncConditionalResult = secondSyncOp(syncConditionalResult);
} else {
  syncConditionalResult = thirdSyncOp(syncConditionalResult);
}

// prints 'Imperative conditional result: 40'
console.log(`Imperative conditional result: ${syncConditionalResult}`);

const asyncConditionalResult = firstAsyncOp()
  .then((val) => {
    if (val > 20) { ②
      return secondAsyncOp(val);
    }
```

213

```
    return val; ③
  })
  .then(thirdAsyncOp);

asyncConditionalResult.then((r) => {
  // prints 'Chained conditional result: 40'
  console.log(`Chained conditional result: ${r}`);
  return r;
});
```

① An imperative conditional check

② We are forced to do the conditional check inside the handler

③ We also need to account for the case where the conditional fails

It is easy to reason about our code when working imperatively—do this if true, else do that. However, things get tricky when using the promise chain—our conditional is embedded inside a handler, wherein we must also accommodate in case the conditional were to fail.

The meat of the argument is that when working with asynchronous code, we are forced to adopt a different programming model as compared to synchronous code. We are not afforded a mechanism to work with asynchronous code in a manner that *seems* imperative, and consequently, we lose out on leveraging most of the facilities that the language offers.

Enter async and await. ES8 introduces two new keywords, with the associated machinery to reduce the difference between synchronous and asynchronous programming models in JavaScript.

# async/await

async, introduced in ES8, is meant to be used as a function modifier. An async function declares to the world that the work being done by the function may be asynchronous. Since our token for asynchronous operations (since ES6) is promises, the previous statement boils down to this—async functions **always** return a promise, like so:

```
const implicitPromise = async () =>
['Implicitly', 'wrapped', 'in', 'a', 'promise']; ①
implicitPromise().then(console.log);
```

```
const explicitPromise = async () =>
  Promise.resolve(['This', 'just', 'returns', 'the', 'promise']); ②
explicitPromise().then(console.log);
```

> ① An async function expression returning a value

> ② An async function returning a promise explicitly

async attempts to reduce the boilerplate by guaranteeing the return of a promise—for functions that simply return a value, the async modifier automatically wraps the return value in a promise. On the other hand, if the function already returns a promise, then it is simply returned.

ES8 simultaneously introduces the await keyword, which can **only** be used within async functions. The role of await is to modify the invocation of a function that happens to return a promise (as opposed to the async keyword that modifies a function *definition*). Since await applies to functions that return promises (which could be other async functions), the role of await is to wait for the promise being returned to be settled and then proceed to unwrap that value. Perhaps the following example will help clear this up:

```
const firstAsyncOp = () => new Promise(res => setTimeout(res, 10, 10)); ①

(async () => { ②
  const result = await firstAsyncOp(); ③
  // prints '10'
  console.log(result);
  return result;
})();
```

> ① A simple function that returns a promise

> ② Define an anonymous async fat-arrow function

> ③ Use await inside the async function to resolve to a value

We start with a function that happens to do its work asynchronously, therefore returning a promise. We then use the await keyword inside an async function to "wait" on the promise being returned to settle and print its result.

The key benefit here is that using await avoids us having to supply a callback to then, which we would have to do to since the result of firstAsyncOp is a promise. Conceptually, await suspends the async function it is wrapped in till the function it is waiting on yields a result. Sounds familiar? This is the same machinery we discussed with generator functions and the `yield` keyword!

Notice how the use of the `await` keyword converts one or more asynchronous calls into imperative, or blocking code. Let us rewrite our earlier example using `async/await` so we can compare the two approaches:

```
const result = (async () => { ①
  const firstAsyncOpResult = await firstAsyncOp(); ②
  const secondAsyncOpResult = await secondAsyncOp(firstAsyncOpResult); ③
  const res = await thirdAsyncOp(secondAsyncOpResult);
  return res; ④
})();

result.then((r) => { ⑤
  console.log('Using async/await', r);
  return r;
});
```

① Define an anonymous `async` fat-arrow function

② Use `await` inside the `async` function to resolve the first operation's value

③ Then proceed to invoke subsequent operations using `await` providing the notion of sequential invocations

④ Finally return the result

⑤ Since `async` operations always return promises, we use `then` to consume the resolved value

We start with our first operation, suspending execution till the promise resolves, and then use that value as an argument to subsequent function calls, eventually returning the fully calculated value. However, when we were previously using promises, we were forced to sequence operations using `then`. `await` eliminates all the ceremony—in fact, this implementation does not look that much different than our synchronous example. The one time where this example does diverge from a synchronous implementation is if we wish to use the `return`-ed value from our IEFE. Recall that the return value from an `async` function is always wrapped in a promise—ergo, if we wish to use result, we are then compelled to use the `then` API.

Leveraging conditionals and looping constructs works just as would expect. Let us return to our earlier example using conditionals, except this time with async/await:

```
const result = (async () => {
  let firstAsyncOpResult = await firstAsyncOp();
  if (firstAsyncOpResult > 20) { ①
    firstAsyncOpResult = await secondAsyncOp(firstAsyncOpResult);
  } else {
    firstAsyncOpResult = await thirdAsyncOp(firstAsyncOpResult);
  }
  return firstAsyncOpResult;
})();

result.then((r) => {
  // prints 'async/await conditional result: 40'
  console.log(`async/await conditional result: ${r}`);
  return r;
});
```

① An imperative conditional check

The fact that firstAsyncOpResult is the result of an *asynchronous* operation in no way affects our code. Take away the async/await keywords and we see that this is exactly how we would work with the results of synchronous operations.

Let us examine a more real-world use-case to highlight the uses of async and await. In this example we will attempt to make an Ajax call using the Fetch API[1] to GET a resource, and unwrap the response. Bear in mind that fetch[2] returns a promise which results in a Response[3] object, which in turn has the json[4] method which too returns a promise. We will write two implementations—one using the native promises, and one using async and await:

```
const getWithPromises = url => fetch(url).then(resp => resp.json()); ①
const getWithAsyncAwait = async (url) => { ②
```

---

[1]https://developer.mozilla.org/en-US/docs/Web/API/Fetch_API
[2]https://developer.mozilla.org/en-US/docs/Web/API/WindowOrWorkerGlobalScope/fetch
[3]https://developer.mozilla.org/en-US/docs/Web/API/Response
[4]https://developer.mozilla.org/en-US/docs/Web/API/Body/json

```
  const resp = await fetch(url); ③
  return await resp.json(); ④
};

const url = 'https://my-json-server.typicode.com/typicode/demo/comments';

getWithPromises(url) ⑤
  .then((json) => {
    console.log(json);
    return json;
  });

getWithAsyncAwait(url) ⑥
  .then((json) => {
    console.log(json);
    return json;
  });

// alternatively
(async () => {
  // either one works just the same
  // const json = await getWithPromises(url);
  const json = await getWithAsyncAwait(url); ⑦
  console.log(json);
})();
```

① Using the native API exposed by fetch

② Define an async function

③ Wait for the fetch operation to complete

④ Then wait for the JSON payload to be resolved

⑤ Invoke our promise-based implementation

⑥ Invoke our async/await-based implementation

⑦ Consume the result of a fetch operation using async/await

This example highlights two subtle but separate concerns. When attempting to use an API (like fetch) that returns promises, using async/await can make the implementation a bit more clearer and easier to reason about. On the flip side, how we implement our fetching functionality has no impact whatsoever on how we consume it. Given that in either case we are always returning a promise, we can either use the traditional then invocation, or use another (anonymous) async function. That is, we can start to consider using async/await any place where we are using a promise chain.

What if a promise were to be rejected? Well, the intent of async/await is to make asynchronous code seem imperative. Therefore, we trap errors (and rejections) the same way we normally do—using our beloved try/catch. Observe:

```
const firstAsyncOp = () =>
  new Promise(res => setTimeout(res, 10, 10)); ①
const secondAsyncOp = arg =>
  new Promise(res => setTimeout(res, 10, arg + 20));
const thirdAsyncOp = () =>
  Promise.reject('Oops!'); ②

const result = (async () => {
  try { ③
    const firstAsyncOpResult = await firstAsyncOp();
    const secondAsyncOpResult = await secondAsyncOp(firstAsyncOpResult);
    const res = await thirdAsyncOp(secondAsyncOpResult);

    return res;
  } catch (e) {
    console.error(e); ④
    return 0;
  }
})();

result.then((r) => {
  // prints '0'
  console.log('Using async/await', r);
  return r;
}); see pg 161
```

① A series of asynchronous operations

② This one is rejected

③ Wrap our code in a try-catch

④ Trap the error just like we would

Our example does not deviate much from our earlier attempts, except this time one of the promises gets rejected. To accommodate for such scenarios, we can wrap our code in a traditional `try/catch` block, trapping errors just like we would have if it were blocking code. In our care our IEFE evaluates to a result, so we simply return 0 (or whatever default makes sense in your case).

As we might conclude, `await` performs two tasks—it suspends the execution of the `async` function till the promise it is waiting on settles, and then unwraps the value that the promised resolved to, allowing the `async` function to continue execution. If the promise were to be rejected, `await` appropriately throws an `Error`, which we can trap using a traditional `try/catch` block. The combination of the two essentially reduces the programming paradigm when working with promises from a functional style to an imperative style. Let us discuss a few more nuances, in particular with regard to `await`, that should shed some light on the best use-cases for the same.

# Nuances and Caveats

First and foremost, it is easy to forget to apply the `await` keyword. This will not result in a syntactical error—however recall that we can only `await` on operations that return promises. If we were to forget to apply the `await` keyword, then we would end up getting a reference to the returned promise, which is not what we want.

Conversely, we can often get carried away with using `await` when we would be better off simply using the promise API. Recall that `await` suspends the execution of the `async` function which bodes well in situations where we need a promise resolved prior to proceeding with subsequent operations. However, in the cases where we can run operations concurrently, we will be better served by dropping down to the promise API, such as `all` or `race`, and consume the results using `await`. Observe:

```
const redundantWaits = (async () => {
  const url = 'https://my-json-server.typicode.com/typicode/demo';
  const fetchPosts = await fetch(`${url}/posts`); ①
  const posts = await fetchPosts.json();

  const fetchComments = await fetch(`${url}/comments`);
```

```
  const comments = await fetchComments.json();

  return {
    posts,
    comments,
  };
})();

redundantWaits
  .then(obj => console.log('From redundantWaits', obj));

const synchronousCalls = (async () => {
  const getJson = url => fetch(url).then(resp => resp.json()); ②

  const url = 'https://my-json-server.typicode.com/typicode/demo';
  const [posts, comments] = await Promise.all([ ③
    getJson(`${url}/posts`),
    getJson(`${url}/comments`),
  ]);

  return {
    posts,
    comments,
  };
})();

synchronousCalls
  .then(obj => console.log('From synchronousCalls', obj));
```

① Wait on each operation in an imperative style

② Simple helper function

③ Run multiple operations concurrently

This time we attempt to accomplish the same task, that is, populating an object with the response from several Ajax calls. However, in this case, the operations do not depend on the output of one another. This is a classic scenario where we should be using the promise APIs to run these tasks concurrently. Of course, like any other function that returns promises, we can always use await to gather up the results of Promise.all and get back in imperative mode.

Another source of potential bugs is if our `async` function relies on some sort of global state.[5] `await` suspends the execution of the function; without blocking the main thread, the runtime can continue working. Therefore, it would be prudent to assume that the global state does not look the same as it did prior to the function being suspended.

That's all for gloomy news. On the sunny side, `await` can consume any object that is then-able—so if we are using some sort of third-party library for promise support, `async` can work with those just as if they were native promises. Go forth! `await` away!

# Summary

`async`/`await`, alongside promises, allow us to approach writing code in JavaScript in a paradigm that best suits our use-case and programming style—the former being rather imperative while the latter promoting more of a functional mindset. While the imperative nature may seem more natural to many of us, we must keep in mind that promises provide us mechanisms like `all` and `race`, that may allow for our code to run faster, but also work with `await`, thereby permitting us to raise or lower the level of abstraction suitable for the problem at hand. The use of promises still has its place, but `await` can certainly help reduce or eliminate some of the tax associated with using promises.

In the next chapter, we will see yet another extension, wherein iterators and generators can now work with asynchronous operations just as easily as they do with synchronous ones.

---

[5]To be fair, this is not the only scenario where relying on global state will lead to bugs :)

# CHAPTER 15

# Asynchronous Iterators and Generators—A Meeting of the Minds

The idea of generators is tempting, and it tends to spoil us. We are no longer afraid to work with large or infinite sequences and streams. However, while generators are great at working with values, they were never designed for working with promises.

In this chapter, we will see yet another reconciliation—one that merges the syntax of generators with `async` and `await`, to give us asynchronous generators, and iterators.

## The Impedance Mismatch Between Generators/ Iterators and Asynchronous Operations

ES6 introduced us to iterables, the well-known symbol `Symbol.iterator` that allows an object to be iterable, as well as the new `for-of` loop that knows to iterate over an iterable. The handshake between an iterator, and anything consuming the iterator, happens to be an object that takes the form `{ value: ..., done: ...}`. If the iterator is not `done`, then the consumer can consume the `value`. Once the return value of the iterator returns `done` to `true`, iteration stops.

ES6 also introduced another feature: generator functions. Generator functions are functions that can be suspended using the `yield` (and `yield*`) operator. They return generator objects that happen to be iterable, which means, they have a method that responds to `Symbol.iterator`. In other words, we can loop over a generator object using the `for-of` loop.

© Raju Gandhi 2019

R. Gandhi, *JavaScript Next*, https://doi.org/10.1007/978-1-4842-5394-6_15

Whatever mechanism we employ to produce or consume iterables will work well if we are operating with the result of synchronous operations. However, if the values happen to be the result of asynchronous operations, or promises, then things become a little arduous. Observe:

```
const randomTimeout = async (val, index) => {
  const timeout = Math.floor(Math.random() * Math.floor(42)); ①
  return new Promise(res =>
    setTimeout(res, timeout, `My value is ${val} at index: ${index}`)); ②
};

const promiseList = [
  randomTimeout(10, 1),
  randomTimeout(20, 2),
  randomTimeout(30, 3),
]; ③

// prints the following (your ordering might vary)
// My value is 20 at index: 2
// My value is 10 at index: 1
// My value is 30 at index: 3
for (const p of promiseList) {
  p.then(console.log); ④
}
```

①A helper function to create a randomized timeout value

②Returns a promise that resolves to a value and an index

③An iterable that contains promises

④We need to wait for the promise to be resolved

We start with a simple helper function that takes a value (to resolve to) and an index so we can see the sequence in which we invoked it. The function implementation produces a random timeout value, and uses that to return a promise that eventually resolves to a value. We then use this helper function to produce an array of asynchronous operations.

Let us, for a moment, ignore the fact that we are using an array of promises, and pretend that the iterable we are working with is of unknown length, like reading all of the lines in a file using I/O. After all, if we had a (fixed) list of promises, we could simply use `Promise.all` to let them work concurrently, and gather up the results.

With that in mind, notice that while the `for-of` loop successfully iterates over the list of promises, we still need to wait for each promise to be resolved. However, the astute observer will notice that this does not fulfill our requirements. While the `for-of` loop diligently returns us the promises in order, they resolve at different times. Therefore, the output we see is not in the same order as the initial order of the promises. That's because the `for-of` loop is not aware that the values being produced by the iterator are asynchronous.

But wait. ES8 introduced us to `async/await`. Can't we use that here? Of course!

```
const promiseList = [
  randomTimeout(10, 1),
  randomTimeout(20, 2),
  randomTimeout(30, 3),
];

(async () => {
  for (const p of promiseList) {
    const res = await p; ①
    console.log(res);
  }
})();
```

      ① `await` out the returned promise prior to proceeding with the loop

This time around, we use `await` to suspend the `for-of` loop till our promise resolves. `await` suspends the execution of the `for-of` till each promise in succession is resolved, thereby giving us the output we expect. We incur the cost of a little boilerplate since we have to wrap the call to `await` inside an anonymous `async` function, but it does seem to work.

Now let us consider the production side. We know that generator functions produce generator objects, which are iterable. Once again, this gets the job done if the values being `yield`-ed are synchronous. But yielding asynchronous data sources produces rather surprising results:

```
function* asyncGenerator() { ①
  yield randomTimeout(10, 1); ②
  console.log('First time');
  yield randomTimeout(20, 2);
  console.log('Second time');
}

const generator = asyncGenerator(); ③
// prints '{ value: Promise { <pending> }, done: false }'
console.log(generator.next());
// prints '{ value: Promise { <pending> }, done: false }'
console.log(generator.next());
// prints '{ value: undefined, done: true }'
console.log(generator.next());

for (const i of asyncGenerator()) {
  console.log(i);
}

(async () => {
  for (const p of asyncGenerator()) {
    const res = await p;
    console.log(res);
  }
})();
```

        ① Define a generator

        ② yield promises

        ③ Start consuming

We define a simple generator, which yields promises, and attempt to get the values by invoking next, then using a traditional for-of loop and finally using async/await. Notice that in each case, we get the expected { value: ..., done: ... } tuple, except in this case, the value happens to be a promise.

This example reveals the true issue at hand—in that, when an iterator hands us a result, it attempts to tell us the value and whether it is done or not. In this case, we see that the `value` happens to be a promise, which may or may not have resolved yet—however, the generator continues to `yield` values till it's done!

In other words, while the resolution of the `value` is asynchronous, the calculation of whether the generator is done *is* synchronous, and therefore, incorrect. We **cannot** declare the iterator to be done till the `value` is resolved (or rejected).

All of this adds salt to the injury—which is, the whole point of iterating over an iterable is to get the values *in sequence*!

To summarize, on the consumption side, we want our `for-of` loops to give us the values we expect in order, pausing for asynchronous data sources to be resolved prior to proceeding to the next iteration.

On the production side, we want to `await` prior to `yield`-ing within a generator. But alas! We can only `await` *inside* `async` functions.

ES9 introduces us to a new symbol, an asynchronous `for-of` loop, and the idea of `async` generators, allowing us to iterate over and produce asynchronous iterables. Let's get started.

# Asynchronous Iterators

We understand the role of `Symbol.iterator`, and how it plays with the `for-of` loop. ES9 introduces us to a new symbol, namely `Symbol.asyncIterator`, which is meant to work for iterables that perform work asynchronously. The contract for any object willing to implement the asynchronous iteration protocol is similar to that of `Symbol.iterator`, in that upon invocation, it must return an object that has a `next` method.

It is here that the implementation diverges from the one for `Symbol.iterator`. Instead of returning an object with the `done` and `value` keys, it should return a promise, that resolves to such an object. Perhaps this is easier seen in code than explained in prose.

```
const fetchFriends = (index) => { ①
  const friends = [
    'Matt',
    'Neal',
    'Ken',
  ];
```

```
  const timeout = Math.floor(Math.random() * Math.floor(42));
  if (index < friends.length) {
    return new Promise(res => setTimeout(res, timeout, friends[index])); ②
  }
  return Promise.reject(new Error('No more records'));
};

class FriendsService { ③
  [Symbol.asyncIterator]() { ④
    let index = 0;
    return { ⑤
      next: async () => { ⑥
        // Make an async call to the backend to retrieve the current
        try {
          const friend = await fetchFriends(index);
            index += 1;
            return { value: friend, done: false }; ⑦
        } catch (e) {
            index = 0;
            return { done: true }; ⑧
        }
      },
    };
  }
}
```

① A simple function that pretends to be a backend call

② And consequently return-s promises with randomized timeouts

③ A simple class

④ Implement Symbol.asyncIterator

⑤ Symbol.asyncIterator returns a simple object, namely the iterator

⑥ The iterator has the next method

⑦ If we have values to return, return the `value` wrapped in
a promise

⑧ Else if we are done iterating return `done:true` wrapped in
a promise

We start by defining a mock database cursor, that uses an index to retrieve a friend from a friends list. To mimic a real-life scenario, we simulate varying retrieval times using a function to generate random timeout values.

This is followed by a simple class that acts a service wrapper around an asynchronous call. In order to adhere to the asynchronous iterability contract, it implements the `Symbol.asyncIterator` method, which returns the iterator. This iterator has the `next` method—however, it does not return a value. Rather, it returns the value wrapped in a promise.

The difference between implementing `Symbol.asyncIterator` and `Symbol.iterator` is that in the case of the former, *both* the `value` and `done` flag are resolved asynchronously.

ES9 also introduces us another `for-of` loop, namely the `for-await-of` loop, which knows how to iterate over asynchronous iterables. This loop, unlike `for-of` loop, knows to `await` out the promise that is returned from the `next` call, before proceeding with the next iteration. As the name suggests, this loop utilizes the `await` keyword, and we know that if we are to use `await`, it must be inside an `async` function. Let us see how we can use this loop with our iterable:

```
(async () => {
  for await (const friend of new FriendsService()) { ①
    console.log(friend);
  }
})();
```

① Use the `for-await-of` loop

Once again, we bear the cost of some boilerplate to wrap the call within an anonymous `async` function, but if we were to run this, we see that our friends show up in the order that they were asked for. The `for-await-loop`, like its counterpart, asks an iterable object for its iterator by invoking the `Symbol.asyncIterator`, then proceeds to invoke the `next` method, `await`-ing the promise that is returned to be resolved, then extracting the `value`. Note that if the `promise` resolves to `done: true`, iteration stops.

We can always choose to invoke the next method ourselves if we choose to, just like with synchronous iterators; however, we will have to append a then call since next invocation return promises.

# Cleaning Up

Asynchronous iterables can do any resource cleanup within its next method prior to signaling an end to the iteration via {done: true}. This works well since it is the iterator that knows it has reached the end.

However, what happens if the for-await-loop were to prematurely stop iteration? Well, just like synchronous iterables, asynchronous iterables can (optionally) implement a return method. This method will be invoked if the client terminates the iteration, like so:

```
class SimpleIterable {
  [Symbol.asyncIterator]() {
    let counter = 0;
    return {
      next: async () => {
        if (counter < 10) {
          counter++;
          return { value: counter, done: false };
        }
          return { done: true };
      },
      async return() { ①
        console.log('Cleaning up');
        return { done: true };
      },
    };
  }
}

(async () => {
  try {
    for await (const n of new SimpleIterable()) { ①
      console.log(n);
```

```
      return; ②
      // or break, or throw new Error()
    }
  } catch (e) {
    console.log('Error', e);
  }
})();
```

① Implement both the required next and optional return method

② Break out prematurely in a for-of loop

We have simplified our earlier example to return a promise that resolves to an incrementing value. But we also implement the return method, which in case simply logs to confirm that we indeed get called. Note that we should signal that the iterable is done as the return value of the return method.

Once again, we find parity between for-await-loop and its peer the for-of loop, in that invoking the return method of the iterable is a side effect of the underlying machinery. That is, the for-await-loop knows to invoke the return method on the iterable if we were to prematurely stop iteration. Other mechanisms to auto-invoke the return method are throw-ing an error within a for-await-of loop, as well as simply break-ing from it.

## Being Imperative

The for-await-of loop lives up to its promise of making asynchronous code look imperative. This facet is accentuated by the mechanism we can use if something were to go wrong. What if the asynchronous iterable that we are looping over were to be rejected? Simple. We can wrap our for-await-loop in a traditional try-catch block. Observe:

```
class SimpleRejectingIterable {
  [Symbol.asyncIterator]() {
    return {
      next: () => Promise.reject('Error!'), ①
    };
  }
}
```

```
(async () => {
  try {
    for await (const n of new SimpleRejectingIterable()) {
      // we will never get here
      console.log(n);
    }
  } catch (e) {
    console.log('Error', e); ②
  }
})();
```

① Reject the promise

② Trap the error using the traditional `try-catch` block

Our iterator in this case simply `reject`-s the promise. If it were to run this example, we will see that `await` unwraps the error, and rightly propagates the error so that the `catch` block catches it. Voila!

## Comingling with Synchronous Iterables

Turns out, the `for-await-of` loop can work with both asynchronous and synchronous iterators. This turns out to be rather beneficial, since we can use it to work even with regular iterables like arrays, maps, and sets. Let us revisit our example of iterating over a list of promises using `for-await-of`:

```
const randomTimeout = async (val, index) => {
  const timeout = Math.floor(Math.random() * Math.floor(42));
  return new Promise(res =>
    setTimeout(res, timeout, `My value is ${val} at index: ${index}`));
  };

const promiseList = [
  randomTimeout(10, 1),
  randomTimeout(20, 2),
  randomTimeout(30, 3),
]; ①
```

```
(async () => {
  for await (const p of promiseList) { ②
    console.log(p);
  }
})();
```

        ① A list of promises

        ② Use the `for-await-of` loop with a synchronous iterable

Allow me to draw your attention to the fact that an array is a synchronous iterable. However, as advertised, the `for-await-of` loop can iterate over it. If the values returned upon each iteration happen to be a promise, the loop is suspended till the value resolves, unwrapped, and handed off to you.

# Generators

We are well aware of the introduction of generators in ES6. As previously discussed, ES6 generators are synchronous. However, what we want when working with asynchronous operations is the ability to `await` prior to yielding—except we cannot `await` without being in an `async` function.

ES9 introduces the ability to apply the `async` keyword to generator functions, in effect, introducing asynchronous generators. We can `await` asynchronous operations within the generator (recall that we only use `await` *inside* of `async` functions) just like we would in regular generators, and once resolved, `yield` those values:

```
const randomTimeout = async (val, index) => {
  const timeout = Math.floor(Math.random() * Math.floor(42));
  return new Promise(res =>
    setTimeout(res, timeout, `My value is ${val} at index: ${index}`));
};

async function* asyncGenerator() { ①
  yield await randomTimeout(10, 1); ②
  console.log('First time');
  yield await randomTimeout(20, 2);
  console.log('Second time');
}
```

```
  console.log(typeof asyncGenerator()[Symbol.asyncIterator] === 'function');

(async () => {
  const gen = asyncGenerator();
  for await (const item of gen) { ③
    console.log('item', item);
  }
})();
```

① Define an `async` generator

② `await` an asynchronous operation

③ Use the `for-await-of` loop to iterate over the generator iterator

An `async` generator, much like a regular generator function, produces an iterator object, except the generator object returned implements the `Symbol.asyncIterator` method (as compared to a synchronous iterable produced by a synchronous generator). Consequently, we can no longer use the `for-of` loop with the generated iterable. However, we *can* use the `for-await-of` loop, since it indeed works with asynchronous iterables.

The machinery for asynchronous generators does not differ from that from synchronous generators. They are mechanisms that allow us to create iterables, permitting for lazy-code, and as a result, create infinite sequences. The difference is in what they return—asynchronous iterators return us iterables that implement the `Symbol.asyncIterator` method, allowing them to be consumed using `for-await-of` loops.

# Parity with Synchronous Iterators and Generators

We have spoken at length about synchronous iterators and generators, specifically about the ability of iterators to implement a `return` method that is invoked if we were to prematurely terminate iteration. We have also seen that generators can act as "consumers," wherein we can influence the next `yield` of the generator by passing an argument to the `next` invocation. All of these apply to asynchronous generators and iterators as well. Finally, recall that the point of `async` and `await` is to make asynchronous operations *seem* imperative. This allows us to wrap the code within an asynchronous generator in a `try-catch` or a `try-catch-finally` block to trap any promises that might be rejected during the execution of the generator.

# Benefits

Asynchronous iterators and generators prove to be useful anytime we wish to consume (lazily or otherwise) the results of asynchronous operations, all while reaping the benefits of the seemingly imperative code that `async/await` offer us. One great example is when reading large files (perhaps using node.js) one line at a time. Another use-case would be consuming APIs where the data returned to us is paginated. Consider Github's API wherein requesting the commits for a repository—Github returns (by default) a 100 commits per response, providing us with a link to the *next* 100 in the response headers. Consuming such an API fits naturally into the facilities offered by asynchronous generators, wherein we `await` every `fetch` and process, and if needed, proceed to the next 100 commits.

# Summary

In this chapter, we saw how ES9's asynchronous iterators and generators allow us to combine `async` and `await` with the on-demand processing capabilities of iterators and generators. This new feature set brings us full circle, incorporating promises, iterators, and generators introduced in ES6, along with `async/await` introduced in ES8, to allow us to work in different contexts at a higher level of abstraction, while bringing parity to synchronous and asynchronous operations.

# Index

© Raju Gandhi 2019
R. Gandhi, *JavaScript Next*, https://doi.org/10.1007/978-1-4842-5394-6